Serve
with
Virginia Wine

Hilde Gabriel Lee and Allan E. Lee

Hildesigns Press
Charlottesville, Virginia

Published by Hildesigns Press
2855 Ridge Road
Charlottesville, Virginia 22901
telephone (804) 296-0885, fax (804) 296-5492

Book design by Hilde G. Lee, Hildesigns
Cover painting © 1994 by Hilde G. Lee

Library of Congress Cataloging in Publication Data
ISBN 0-9639605-1-2

Printed in the United States of America

CONTENTS

INTRODUCTION

This book is a sequel to *Virginia Wine Country Revisited* that was published by Hildesigns Press in 1993. Many of the vintners described in that book told us that visitors to their tasting rooms frequently asked about recipes that would go with the vintner's wines. The idea of a book that would provide recipes to accompany various Virginia wines grew out of those comments. In the spring of 1993 we decided to create this book by identifying all of the varietal wines produced in Virginia and developing recipes that complement these wines. Few Virginia wine lovers realize that there are 37 different varietal wines being produced in Virginia, plus champagne.

The recipes were all created by Hilde, who kept their affinity with wine in mind. The recipes tend to be light, both in texture and ingredients, in recognition of the modern trend toward healthier cuisine. This approach fits well with Virginia wines as they tend to be light-to-moderate in body. Hilde is a recognized food authority, having written seven nationally distributed books on cooking, been on radio and television food-related talk shows, and has been the featured food columnist in the Charlottesville Daily Progress for more than six years.

Our focus on varietal wines of Virginia does not mean that we are ignoring the many fine blended wines being produced by Virginia vintners. Blends are hard to describe in the sense of relating them to specific food recipes. The melding of varietal characteristics inherent in blended wines makes the description of their taste and olfactory sensations difficult. In addition, vintners change the base wines and their mix each year, depending on the results of the year's harvest. Comments on one year's blended wines, therefore, do not necessarily apply to previous or following vintages.

We have included at least one recipe for each of the 19 varietal white wines, 18 red wines, and champagne. Most have two or more recipes. The recipes having an affinity with Chardonnay have been divided into two categories, those that are best complemented by an oaked Chardonnay and those that can best be enjoyed with a more austere non-oaked Chardonnay.

The assignment of a particular recipe to a specific wine does not mean that that recipe would not be as good, or even better, with another wine. Given the diversity of wines in Virginia, it proved to be a difficult task for us to provide a recipe suggestion for each and every wine. The selections should, therefore, be considered as merely that, suggestions. The reader should pair the recipe with wine he or she has come to like. As has been stated frequently by wine writers and experts, "While there are general guidelines as to what wine goes with what food components, the best selection of a wine is the one that goes best for your own taste." One top California vintner is found of saying, "I love my Cabernet and drink it with everything, whether meat, fish, or fowl."

We wish to thank all of the vintners who contributed their time and furnished material for inclusion in this book. Many of them were instrumental in urging us to write the book, based on their own interest in having Virginia wines paired with food. We also want to thank Christine Koontz of Barboursville Vineyards who graciously allowed us to use her pictures of grapes she photographed in the vineyard. The still life painting on the cover was done by HIlde, who also painted the cover for *Virginia Wine Country Revisited.*

We hope you will enjoy this accompaniment to *Virginia Wine Country Revisited.* Each book is meant to be enjoyed by itself, but together they provide a full exposure to what the Virginia wine industry has to offer. The recipes in this book will provide many enjoyable meals. In addition to American, the recipes include a wide range of ethnic dishes, including Chinese, German, Italian, Middle Eastern, and Hungarian, among others.

We hope your experience in pairing food with Virginia wine will enhance your appreciation of Virginia wines and your enjoyment of wine with food, generally.

Hilde and Allan Lee
September, 1994

THE WINE GRAPES OF VIRGINIA

Three basic strains of wine grapes can currently be found growing in Virginia. The strain with the longest pedigree includes the Native American varieties that were growing here when the first settlers arrived. Next came the French Hybrids, which arrived in North America around World War II, but were not planted in Virginia until the 1960s. The most recently planted strain consists of the European-style *Vitis Vinifera* varieties, which were first successfully planted in Virginia, and the eastern United States generally, in the 1970s. The early colonists and settlers in Virginia had tried for almost two centuries to cultivate *Vitis Vinifera,* but without success due to their inability to cope with pests and climatic conditions.

American Natives

The strains of native American grapes are generally further classified into two categories, the purely native American species, which were growing in the region along the eastern seaboard when the white man first arrived in North America, and the American hybrid varieties that are cross-breeds of native American species with European *Vinifera* species. This hybridizing occurred either naturally in the wild over several hundred years as settlers made experimental plantings of *Vinifera* vines nearby, or it was consciously undertaken by man in an attempt to improve on nature. Most of the hybrid American varieties deliberately cross-bred by man were developed during the second half of the 1800s.

The pure native American species are no longer found in commercial wines of Virginia, except for the Scuppernong grape of the *Vitis Rotundifolia* species. Among the naturally cross-bred American varieties still cultivated today are the Catawba, Concord, Isabella, and Delaware varieties. Among the man-created varieties being grown today are the Norton (Cynthia), Niagara, and Steuben.

French Hybrids

Americans were not the only hybridizers during the late 1800s. French vineyards had been hit with a disastrous attack of phylloxera and other diseases, which nearly destroyed the French wine industry. The immediate solution was to replant the vineyards with Native American varieties such as Isabella, Clinton, Noah, or Othello. These American natives did not do well in France and were quickly replaced with European *Vitis Vinifera* varieties grafted onto the more disease-resistant native American root stocks such as *Riparia, Rupestris,* or *Labrusca* families. French vineyardists imported millions of American root stocks during the

Seyval, a French hybrid

late 1800s and early 1900s. This approach proved successful and is used throughout the world today.

Grafting is a labor-intensive and expensive process, however. So soon after the phylloxera epidemic, French hybridizers started experimenting with cross-breeding European and American varieties. They hoped to develop new hybrids that would have the hardy American root stock while retaining the delicate wine characteristics of the European *Vinifera* varieties. Hybridizers created hundreds of thousands of crosses, out of which only a dozen or so yielded wine with commercial potential. Those that succeeded proved to be disease resistant and highly productive. While making good table wine, however, these hybrids do not, in general, yield the truly fine characteristics of the pure European *Vinifera* varieties.

Since they are easy to grow, French vineyardists immediately started planting thousands of acres of hybrids. They became so popular as everyday house wines that France was in danger of losing its world-wide reputation for fine wines. The government finally stepped in and sharply restricted the planting of the French hybrids in France. Acreage of hybrids in France reached its peak in 1958, although hybrid acreage in France still exceeds the total acreage of wine grapes grown in California today.

Commercial winemaking in the United States ceased during prohibition and was slow to redevelop in the 1930s. While the California wine industry had become relatively well-established by the mid-1940s, interest in commercial winemaking in eastern North America did not materialize until after World War II. During the 1930s and 1940s winemaking in the eastern part of the country was limited to a few innovative vineyardists, plus researchers at universities and agricultural stations in New York, Pennsylvania, and Maryland who experimented with native and French hybrids. Virginia did not participate to any noticeable extent in this research as the state was still under the influence of the prohibitionists.

Following World War II consumer interest in wine began to accelerate, which stimulated the increase in research and the planting of commercial vineyards—particularly in New York state. Eastern researchers and commercial vineyardists obtained cuttings of French hybrids via Canada as the federal Department of Agriculture was slow to permit their entry from Europe. Additional plantings of these French hybrids continued through the 1950s and into the 1960s. The first commercial vineyards of French hybrids appeared in Virginia in the late 1960s.

Vitis Vinifera

Production of French hybrid wine grapes continued to expand in the United States into the late 1980s. However, market forces in the major urban areas began pressuring eastern vineyardists and wineries to produce European-style wines. Hence, eastern vintners began experimenting with cultivation of *Vinifera* grapes in the 1960s and 1970s. By then, American chemical technology had developed the necessary pesticides and fungicides that overcame the problem encountered by the colonists and settlers.

Modern agricultural technology prevailed and the first successful commercial planting of *Vinifera* grapes in Virginia occurred in the early 1970s. By 1980 Virginia acreage of *Vinifera* grapes had exceeded that of French hybrids. Today, *Vinifera* varieties of wine grapes in Virginia account for three quarters of the total grown. Within the *Vinifera* family, the three most popular in Virginia are Chardonnay, Cabernet Sauvignon, and Riesling, with Chardonnay representing 40 percent of the total *Vinifera*. Merlot and Cabernet Franc appear to do well in Virginia and plantings of these varieties are increasing rapidly.

Malvasia, a Vitis Vinifera

Other important *Vinifera* varieties presently being grown in Virginia include Sauvignon Blanc, Pinot Noir, and Gewürtztraminer. Recently, vintners have begun to plant varieties found in the Rhone Valley of France and in northern Italy. Rhone varieties include Viognier and Marsanne, while Italian varieties include Pinot Grigio, Sangiovese, Malvasia, Trebbiano, and Moscato. Today, Virginia vintners are cultivating approximately 45 different varieties of wine grapes, of which 26, or 58 percent, are from the *Vitis Vinifera* family. Of the 45-variety total, the vintners consider the quality of the grapes sufficiently high to make varietal wines from 37 varieties, of which 24 are *Vinifera*, 8 are French hybrids, and 5 are American hybrids.

GRAPE VARIETIES GROWN BY VIRGINIA VINTNERS

(Wineries not listed if over twelve)

White Grapes

Cayuga (4) — Mtn Cove, Rose Rvr, Stonewall, Farelu

Chardonnay (36)

Chenin Blanc (2) — Afton, Simeon

Delaware (1) — Meredyth

Gewurztraminer (6) — Afton, Barboursville, Loudoun, Oasis, Rapidan, Rebec

Malvaxia ((2) — Barboursville, Villa Appalaccia

Marsanne (1) — Horton

Moscato (2) — Barboursville, Villa Appalaccia

Niagara (1) — Morrisette

Pinot Gris (Grigio) (3) — Barboursville, Jefferson, Tarara

Ravat (1) — Rose River

Riesling (24)

Sauvignon Blanc (6) — Barboursvillle, Jefferson, Linden, Loudoun, Naked Mountain,

Scheurube (1) — Loudoun

Sémillon (2) — Afton, Piedmont,

Seyval (15)

Steuben (1) — Deer Meadow

Trebbiano (1) — Villa Appalaccia

Veltliner (1) — Loudoun

Vidal Blanc (18)

Villard Blanc (2) — Meredyth, Mtn Cove

Viognier (2) — Tarara, Horton

Red Grapes

Baco Noir (2) — Burnley, Mountain Cove

Barbera (1) — Barboursville

Cabernet Franc (19)

Cabernet Sauvignon (31)

Chambourcin (12) — Burnley, Deer Meadow, Guilford, Hartwood, Ingleside, Morrisette, North Mtn, Oakencroft, Rockbridge, Shenandoah, Stonewall, Swedenburg

Chancellor (3) — Farelu, Mtn Cove, Rose Bower

Chelois (1) — Guilford

de Chaunac (3) — Burnley, Farfelu, Meredyth,

Gamay (1) — Loudoun

Malbec (1) — Horton

Maréchal Foch (5) — Burnley, Deer Meadow, Meredyth, North Mtn, Rose Bower

Merlot (11) — Afton, Ch. Morrisette, Hartwood, Horton, Ingleside, L. Anna, Misty Mtn, Oasis, Rapidan, Simeon, Totier, Williamsburg

Mourvedre (1) — Horton

Nebbiolo (1) — Loudoun

Norton (1) — Horton

Petit Verdot (1) — Prince Michel

Pinot Noir (10) — Barboursville, Ch. Morrisette, Hartwood, Ingleside, Jefferson, Loudoun, Rebec, Rose Bower, Tarara

Rayon d'Or (1) — Guilford

Rougeon (1) — North Mountain

Sangiovese (3) — Jefferson, Loudoun, Villa Appalacia

Syrah (1) — Horton

Villard Noir (1) — Mountain Cove

Zinfandel (3) — Afton, Loudoun, Jefferson

VARIETAL WINES PRODUCED IN VIRGINIA

(x) *Indicates number of wineries producing each varietal wine.*
Wineries not listed if ten or more.

White Wines

Cayuga (1) — Stonewall
Chardonnay (36)
Chenin Blanc (2) — Afton, Jefferson
Delaware (1) — Meredyth
Gewürztraminer (6) — Afton, Barbours-
   ville, Oasis, Pr. Michel, Rebec,
   Shenendoah
Malvasia (1) — Barboursville
Marsanne (1) — Horton
Moscato (2) — Barboursville, Villa
   Appalaccia
Niagara (1) — Ch. Morrisette
Pinot Grigio (Gris (2) — Barboursville,
   Jefferson
Riesling (21)
Sauvignon Blanc (5) — Barboursville,
   Jefferson, Linden, Naked Mountain,
   Shenedoah
Sémillon (2) — Afton, Piedmont
Seyval Blanc (11)
Steuben (1) — Deer Meadow
Trebbiano (1) — Villa Appalaccia
Vidal Blanc (14)
Villard Blanc (1) — Mountain Cove
Viognier (1) — Horton

Red Wines

Baco Noir (1) — Mountain Cove
Barbera (1) — Barboursville
Cabernet Franc (6) — Barboursville,
   Horton, Jefferson, Oasis, Tarara,
   Willowcroft
Cabernet Sauvignon (30)
Chambourcin (5) — Burnley, Chateau
   Morrisette, Deer Meadow, North Mtn.,
   Stonewall
de Chaunac (1) — Meredyth
Gamay Beaujolais (1) — Loudoun
Malbec (1) — Horton
Maréchel Foch (3) — Deer Meadow,
   Meredyth, Rose Bower
Merlot (12)
Mourvedre (1) — Horton
Nebbiolo (1) — Loudoun
Norton (1) — Horton
Pinot Noir (7) — Afton, Barboursville,
   Ch Morrisette, Jefferson, Loudoun,
   Rockbridge, Tarara
Sangiovese (2) — Jefferson, Loudoun
Syrah (1) — Horton
Villard Noir (1) — Meredyth
Zinfandel (2) — Afton, Loudoun

Champagne (Sparkling Wine) (5) —
Barboursville, Ingleside, Oasis,
Prince Michel, Rose Bower

WINERIES PRODUCING VARIETAL WINES IN VIRGINIA

Winery	Chard'y	Cab Sauv	Riesling	Seyval	Vidal	Merlot	Others
Afton Mountain	x	x	x			x	Chenin Blanc, Sémillon, P. Noir, G'ztraminer, Zinfandel
Autumn Hill	x	x	x				
Barboursville	x	x	x			x	Sauv Blanc, G'ztraminer, Barbera, Cab Franc, P. Noir, Malvasia, Champagne, Moscato
Burnley	x	x	x				Chambourcin
Chateau Morrisette	x	x		x	x		P. Noir, Niagara, Chambourcin
Deer Meadow	x	x		x	x		Chambourcin, Foch, Steuben
Dominion							
Farfelu	x	x					
Gray Ghost	x	x			x		Cayuga
Guilford Ridge							
Harwood	x	x	x	x	x		
Hollerith	x						
Horton					x		Cab Franc, Malbec, Marsanne, Mouvèdre, Norton, P. Grigio, Syrah, Viognier
Ingleside	x	x			x		Champagne
Jefferson	x	x	x			x	Cab Franc, P. Noir, P. Grigio, Sangiovese, Sauv Blanc
Lake Anna	x	x		x		x	Sauv Blanc
Linden	x	x		x			
Loudoun Valley	x	x	x				Zinfandel, Nebbiolo, Sangiovese
Meredyth	x	x	x	x		x	Foch, de Chaunac, Delaware
Misty Mountain.	x	x	x			x	
Montdomaine	x	x				x	
Mountain Cove							Villard Blanc, Baco Noir
Naked Mtn.	x	x	x				Sauv Blanc

Winery	Chard'y	Cab Sauv	Riesling	Seyval	Vidal	Merlot	Other Varietal Wines
North Mountain	x						Chambourcin
Oakencroft	x	x			x		
Oasis	x	x	x	x	x	x	G'ztraminer, Cab Franc, Champagne
Piedmont	x	x		x			Sémillon
Pr. Michel/Rapidan	x	x	x			x	G'ztraminer, Champagne
Rebec	x	x	x		x		G'ztraminer
Rockbridge	x		x		x		Pinot Noir
Rose Bower	x		x	x	x		Foch, Champagne
Rose River	x	x	x		x		
Shenandoah	x	x	x			x	G'ztraminer, Sauv Blanc, P.Noir
Stonewall					x		Cayuga, Chambourcin
Swedenburg	x	x	x	x			
Tarara	x	x					P. Noir, Cab Franc
Tomahawk Mill	x						
Totier Creek	x	x	x			x	
Villa Appalaccia					x		Trebbiano, Malvasia, Moscato, Cab Franc
Williamsburg	x	x				x	
Willowcroft	x	x	x	x			Cab Franc
Wintergreen	x	x	x				
TOTAL	36	31	21	11	14	12	(See next page for totals of other wines)

WINERIES PRODUCING VARIETAL WINES IN VIRGINIA — continued

OTHER WINES: (Number of wineries offering varietal wine)

Cabernet Franc	7	Sangiovese	2
Pinot Noir	7	Sémillon	2
Gewürztraminer	6	Zinfandel	2
Sauvignon Blanc	5	Baco Noir	1
Champagne	5	Barbera	1
Chambourcin	5	Cayuga	1
Maréchel Foch	3	Chenin Blanc	1
Malvasia	2	de Chaunac	1
Moscato	2	Delaware	1
Pinot Grigio	2	Malbec	1
Marsanne	1		
Mouvèdre	1		
Nebbiola	1		
Niagara	1		
Norton	1		
Steuben	1		
Syrah	1		
Villard Blanc	1		
Villard Noir	1		
Viognier	1		

FOOD AND WINE PAIRING

Many of us are frustrated with the seemingly formidable task of properly matching food and wine. Making these decisions with confidence sometimes appears to involve mystical riddles that defy the best efforts of both the right and left side of our brains.

Perhaps we take the task too seriously as all we are trying to do is enhance our enjoyment of two delightful experiences, eating a good meal and drinking enjoyable wine. This is not a life-threatening activity, and besides, there is a wide range of good wines that can be enjoyed with any given food dish. Unless the objective of your dinner party is specifically to evaluate various food and wine selections, your guests are more likely to appreciate the quality of the wine rather than its degree of affinity with the food on their plates.

Before going further, it is helpful to know something about the nature of wine and its effect on your senses. Most of us do not stop to reflect on the fact that nearly half our reaction to a wine comes from the olfactory senses (Try enjoying wine while holding your nose), so the aromas given off by the wine are important to its enjoyment. Second, as the wine enters your mouth, five elements of taste immediately become significant: acidity, sweetness, bitterness, alcohol, and fruitiness. A balanced wine is one that none of the first four elements predominate in the first instance, which allows the fruit-related flavors of the wine to come forward.

Acidity gives the wine freshness and crispness, although too much gives the wine a residual sour taste. High acid wines go well with a wide range of foods, particularly those that are salty (ham), oily (fish), rich (cream sauces) or acidic (tomatoes). Conversely, low-acid wines are swamped by acidic foods.

Sweetness in wine comes, of course, from the residual sugar remaining in the wine after fermentation. In table wine, this can range from essentially zero percent to 10 percent. Dry wine is defined as having less than 0.5 percent residual sugar, off-dry up to 1.5 percent, semisweet up to 3 percent, and sweet more than 3 percent residual sugar. Generally speaking, dry wine has affinity with a wider range of foods than do the sweeter styles. Off-dry and semisweet wines can complement foods that also have sweet components. Sweet wines, of course, are most enjoyable with rich desserts. The general rule, however, is that the food should have somewhat less sweetness than the wine to avoid having the flavors of the food wipe out that of the wine.

The third element, bitterness, is derived from the tannin in the wine. Tannin is encountered mostly in red grapes, since their skins and stems are heavier in tannin than those of white wine grapes. Also, the wine is typically left on the skins and stems during crushing and fermentation, allowing it to pick up more tannin. Wine aged in new barrels also picks up tannin from that source. While the taste of tannin is not a pleasant one, it does dissipate with age and helps preserve the wine during the aging process. When pairing wine with food, keep

in mind that a tannic wine does help cut through the fattiness of meat and cheese. Since tannin leaves a bitter taste in the mouth, tannic red wines, particularly young ones, should not accompany bitter foods.

Alcohol, the fourth element, is created during the fermentation process from the natural sugar contained in the grape. Most table wines contain from 11.5-12.5 percent alcohol with 14 percent being the legal maximum. High alcohol content is caused by high sugar content in the grapes at the time of harvest. Some German Rieslings have developed very little sugar by harvest time and the wine ends up with as low as 8 percent alcohol. Since alcohol is dense (heavy), a high percentage of alcohol in the wine produces a heavy-bodied wine. It also produces a somewhat unpleasant "hot" sensation as the wine touches the tongue. Alcoholic wines go best with rich country-style foods. Conversely, wines with low alcohol are light-bodied and go best with light foods. Alcohol gives a sensation of sweetness and wines with high alcohol do not go well with dishes having a sweet component.

Fruitiness is a confusing term to most wine drinkers as it does not necessarily mean the wine tastes like fruit. Rather, it refers to the presence of aromas and tastes that are characteristic of the varietal grape when freshly-crushed. The berry-like aromas and flavors of many young red wines are relatively easy to match with a range of foods, while some white wines that have undertones of melon and pineapple are more difficult because they give a sensation of sweetness. Certain wines, such as Sauvignon Blanc have a vegetal rather than fruity character, which goes well with vegetable dishes, spicy foods, and fish dishes.

Fruitiness disappears as the wine matures with age. Mature red wines develop an earthy character, which is particularly noticeable in a mature Pinot Noir wine. Red meat, mushrooms, and earthy vegetables make a particularly interesting match with such wines.

With this discussion of the nature of wine in mind, there are general rules that we can rely on to make enjoyable pairings. The first rule is to realize that the principle ingredient in a dish does not always dictate the type and style of the most suitable wine. Chicken can be complemented by either a red or white wine, depending on whether it is grilled or cooked in the oven, and whether it is merely seasoned or is smothered in a sauce. The more severe the cooking heat, and the more spicy or acidic the sauce, the more full-bodied the wine needed.

The often-heard rule that white wines should be served with fish and red wines with red meat is no longer a reliable one. These rules were effective when food dishes were of the meat-and-potatoes variety, and wines were aggressive in character. Today, dishes have become complex, having layers of aromas and tastes. Coupled with this, wines have also become more complex and subtle. So the true wine/food aficionado learns to match the over-riding flavors of the food with those of the wine.

The acidity of a wine is more important than its color when pairing with food. A highly-acid, light-bodied red wine can better complement a fish dish, for example, than a flabby or sweet white wine. Acidity cuts the oil in the fish in the same way lemon juice does. In general, red wine goes better with fish when the fish has been "browned." Fish and heavily-oaked wines, such as Cabernet and some Chardonnays, do not go well together as the oak overwhelms the taste of the fish. The combination of sweet wines with fish is also a downer, unless there is a sweet element in the sauce.

When serving most shell fish dishes we prefer to stay with a dry white wine such as Sauvignon Blanc. This wine provides a herbaceous sensation, which complements the complex flavors of the shell fish. Sauvignon Blanc also goes well with seasoned Indian and Mexican dishes.

Red wine with red meat is still an effective general rule unless the meat is covered with a cream sauce. White meats, such as chicken or veal, can be enjoyed with a white wine, unless the meat is accompanied by a heavily-spiced sauce. As with fish, browned white meats can be enjoyed with a light- or moderate-bodied red wine. Well-cooked red meat, such as in a stew, can be accompanied by a white wine with good fruit and acid, such as an oaked Chardonnay.

The same general rules apply with pasta, which tends to be rather neutral with respect to wine. Wine selection depends on the sauce and other ingredients that are melded with the pasta in the dish. Pasta in tomato sauce requires an acidic wine, preferable a mature one, because tomato sauce and fruity wines tend to fight each other.

Deciding what wine to serve with a salad leads most chefs to serve none. The typical oil and vinegar dressings simply overpower most wines. One solution is to substitute lemon juice or a high-acid wine for the vinegar, or use a very mild vinegar. It helps to have wine-friendly ingredients in the salad such as fruit, vegetables, cheese, meat, and/or nuts. In any case, an acidic white wine is usually preferred.

For those of you who like to serve cheese for dessert, the general rule is that red wine goes best with firm cheeses, while a spicy, sweet white wine tends to be most compatible with soft cheese. One exception is that Camembert can be enjoyed with an aged Cabernet or Merlot. The fat in most soft cheeses cancels the tannins in younger red wines and makes them flabby.

Champagne is inherently a high acid wine, and, coupled with the effervescense of the bubbles, can be paired with a wide range of foods, from appetizers to desserts. It comes with varying amounts of residual sugar and the same rules regarding sugar in still wines also applies to champagne. Refer to the recipe section on champagne for further discussion of pairing champagne with food.

WHITE WINES

Cayuga

First released in 1972, Cayuga is a white American hybrid that was developed at the Geneva Experiment Station in New York state. Its parents include Seyval and Zinfandel. The Cayuga vines are good producers, are resistant to many diseases, but are only moderately winter hardy. Wine from the Cayuga grape has a delicate, fruity flavor with a pleasant aftertaste.

Currently, Stonewall Vineyards near Appomatox and Farfelu Vineyard in northern Virginia are the only growers and producers of Cayuga wine in Virginia. The winemaker at Stonewall, Bart Davis, makes his Cayuga in an off-dry German style. Davis enhances the fruitiness of the wine by cold fermenting it. Charles Raney, owner of Farfelu, adds 10 percent Chardonnay to his dry Cayuga-based wine which he calls Dry Picnic White.

Parsnip and Orange Soup

The slight sweetness of the parsnips and the orange flavor in this English soup complement the citrus-like fruitiness of the Cayuga varietal wine.

Serves 6

2 tablespoons butter or margarine
1 medium onion, chopped
1 medium potato, peeled and diced
2 pounds parsnips, peeled and diced
4 cups chicken broth

½ cup orange juice
Rind of ½ orange, cut in wide strips
¼ teaspoon pepper
½ cup whipping cream

Melt the butter in a large saucepan, and add the onion, potato, and parsnips. Cook, covered, over low heat until the vegetables are softened, about 10 minutes. Add the chicken broth, orange juice, orange rind, and pepper. Simmer, covered, for 20 to 25 minutes or until the vegetables are done. Transfer the solids to the bowl of a food processor and puree. If a finer texture is desired push the mixture through a fine sieve. Return the puree to the saucepan and incorporate it with the liquid. Stir in the cream, heat through, and serve.

Herbed Rock Cornish Game Hens

Fresh or dried herbs may be used in this easy-to-prepare dish. Serve with a pasta salad for a company barbecue.

Serves 6

2 tablespoons fresh oregano leaves or
    2 teaspoons dried
2 tablespoons fresh thyme leaves or
    2 teaspoons dried
2 tablespoons fresh rosemary leaves or
    2 teaspoons dried
2 tablespoons fresh chopped sage or
    ½ teaspoon dried

3 garlic cloves, chopped
½ teaspoon salt
¼ teaspoon pepper
½ cup lemon juice
¼ cup extra-virgin olive oil
3 large (about 1 ½ pounds each) Rock
    Cornish game hens

If using fresh herbs chop them finely. Combine the herbs with the garlic, salt, pepper, and lemon juice. Whisk in the oil.

Place the Cornish hens in a dish large enough to hold them in one layer. Ladle the herb mixture over them. Place in the refrigerator and let the hens marinate for at least 6 hours, turning them once.

Drain the hens and reserve the marinade. Grill them over charcoal on a rack set 5 to 6 inches above the glowing coals for about 40 minutes or until done. During cooking, baste the hens with the marinade every 15 minutes.

Pork Piccata

Inspired by the classic Italian veal piccata recipe, this dish is made with pork tenderloin. The capers and the hint of lemon pair well with Cayuga.

Serves 4 to 6

1 ½ pounds pork tenderloin, cut
    crosswise into 12 slices
Flour combined with salt and pepper,
    for dredging
2 tablespoons butter or margarine
2 tablespoons olive oil

½ cup dry white wine
¼ cup lemon juice
2 tablespoons capers
3 tablespoons finely chopped parsley
1 teaspoon dried basil
1 teaspoon dried thyme

Pound the pork slices between two sheets of plastic wrap to flatten them (about 1/4 inch thick). Dredge the pork slices lightly in the flour and shake off the excess.

Heat 1 tablespoon of the butter and 1 tablespoon of the olive oil in a large skillet over medium-high heat. Add half of the pork slices and sauté them for 2 minutes on each side or until just done. Transfer the pork slices to a warm platter and keep them warm. Melt the remaining butter with the olive oil and sauté the rest of the pork slices. Remove them from and pan and keep warm.

Add the wine to the skillet and deglaze over high heat, scraping up any brown bits. Reduce the liquid by half. Add the lemon juice, capers, parsley, basil, and thyme, stirring the mixture well. Reduce heat to medium low and cook just long enough to warm the sauce. Pour the sauce over the pork slices and serve immediately.

Chardonnay

Chardonnay is the classical white wine of the Burgundy, Chablis, and Champagne regions of France. Easy to grow, it is probably the most popular fine white wine in the world today. The Chardonnay grape is one of the most versatile wine grapes in existence as the wine can be produced in a variety of styles, from a flinty austere wine to a full-bodied complex one. Chardonnay is almost universally fermented dry.

The grape's basic fruity character produces an appley flavor with undertones of vanilla, pineapple, and various tropical fruits. While it is thoroughly enjoyable as a simple wine fermented and aged in temperature controlled stainless steel tanks, most vintners today give their Chardonnay additional complexity through a combination of fermentation and/or aging in oak barrels. Of the white wines, Chardonnay has the greatest affinity to oak aging.

Oak treatment of the wine is handled in four ways — fermenting and/or aging the wine in oak barrels, varying the amount of time the wine is allowed to spend in oak barrels, fermenting or aging only a portion of the wine in oak, and varying the type and age of oak barrels used. New barrels provide a more intense oakiness than do barrels that have had several years of use. In general, French oak barrels currently yield more subtle flavors to the wine than do barrels made from American oak. French-made barrels have become extremely expensive, so American vintners are making greater use of American oak barrels, the quality of which has improved in recent years.

Vintners also often create a softer and buttery tone to Chardonnay by allowing the wine to proceed through malolactic (also referred to as secondary) fermentation. Malolactic fermentation converts the naturally occurring malic acid in the grape juice into softer lactic acid, a distinguishing acid in dairy products. While a common process with many red wines, Chardonnay is typically the only white wine to undergo secondary fermentation due to its unusually high acidity.

When consumed with food, Chardonnay is most enjoyable with a modest amount of contact with oak. Chardonnay that has been fermented and aged only in stainless steel tanks, that is, not coming in contact with oak, can be a very pleasing wine, particularly with light salads and hors d'oeuvres. An overly-oaked Chardonnay can lose much of the natural flavor of the grape, while the harsh taste of excess oak clashes with that of the food.

In Virginia, all but a few vintners offer at least one style of Chardonnay. A number offer at least two styles, and several of the largest wineries even produce three types. The three most common styles marketed by Virginia wineries are: an austere stainless steel-only fermented and aged style, a stainless fermented coupled with barrel aging style, and a style that is both fermented and aged in oak barrels. Virginia vintners using grapes with unusually-high acidity will frequently allow the wine to go through secondary fermentation, particularly wines that have been aged in oak barrels.

Almost all early attempts at making Chardonnay in Virginia produced a simple, somewhat austere wine of varying quality. Virginia Chardonnay vines have matured over the past two decades, however, and Virginia vintners have learned how to stabilize their wines through use of temperature-controlled tanks and careful filtering. Today Virginia vintners produce world-class Chardonnay in a wide variety of styles, from a simple fruity light style to a more complex, oaky style with buttery overtones.

Stainless Chardonnay

Avocados Filled with Seafood

These stuffed avocado halves may be served as an appetizer or as a main course. If small bay shrimp are not available, substitute cooked medium shrimp and cut them into bite-size pieces.

Serves 4 as an appetizer or 2 as a main course

2 avocados
½ pound crabmeat
¼ pound bay shrimp (or cooked medium shrimp)
¼ cup minced celery
2 tablespoons minced red pepper

1 teaspoon lemon juice
3 tablespoons mayonnaise
¼ teaspoon curry powder
Lettuce leaves
2 hard-boiled eggs, chopped
Paprika

Cut the avocados in half, peel, and remove the seed. Pick over the crabmeat to remove any cartilage and combine with the shrimp, celery, and red pepper in a bowl. Sprinkle with the lemon juice. Combine the mayonnaise and curry powder and mix with the seafood. If the mixture is not moist enough, add a little more mayonnaise and a dash more curry powder, to taste.

Place the avocado halves on lettuce leaves. Spoon the crabmeat mixture into and over the avocado halves. Sprinkle each half with some chopped egg and dust with paprika before serving.

Sweet Potato Soup

Sweet potatoes have always been a popular vegetable in Virginia. In this recipe they are combined with corn and chili peppers for a soup with a Southwestern flavor. The fruitiness of a stainless-steel fermented Chardonnay complements the sweetness and slight spiciness of this soup.

Serves 4

2 tablespoons butter or margarine
1 medium onion, chopped
1 ½ pounds sweet potatoes peeled and
    cut in large cubes
¼ teaspoon pepper
5 cups chicken broth (or half canned
    chicken broth and half water)

1 ¾ cups fresh corn kernels or frozen
    corn kernels, thawed
⅓ cup chopped red bell pepper
1 jalapeño pepper, seeded and finely chopped
1 teaspoon chopped fresh oregano,
    or ½ teaspoon dried oregano
Fresh cilantro leaves, for garnish

Melt the butter in a medium-size saucepan, add the onion and sauté the onion until limp, but not brown. Add the sweet potatoes, pepper, and chicken broth. Bring to a boil and cook, covered, over low heat for 25 to 30 minutes, or until the potatoes are tender.

Strain the soup and puree the solids in a food processor. (A hand-held blender may also be used to puree the solids in the saucepan.) Return the liquid and puree to the saucepan and add the corn, red pepper, jalapeño pepper, and oregano. Bring to a slow boil and simmer 5 to 7 minutes until the corn is tender. Ladle into soup bowls and garnish with cilantro leaves.

Green Salad with Hazelnuts

Salads which traditionally contain vinegar in the dressing do not pair well with wine. However, this green salad, flavored with hazelnuts, uses wine in the dressing and can be served with a white wine. The tartness of the watercress is contrasted by the sweetness of the mustard in the salad dressing. If hazelnut oil is not available use two types of olive oil.

Serves 6

1 bunch red lettuce, washed, dried,
    and torn into bite-sized pieces
1 head butter lettuce, washed, dried,
    and torn into bite-sized pieces
1 bunch watercress, washed, dried,
    and coarse stems removed
⅓ cup dry white wine

1 ¼ tablespoons hot, sweet mustard
⅛ teaspoon salt
¼ teaspoon white pepper
¼ cup hazelnut oil
¼ cup olive oil
1 ¼ cup hazelnuts, lightly toasted and coarsely chopped

Combine the lettuces and watercress in a large bowl. Whisk together the wine, mustard, salt, and pepper. Slowly whisk in the oils until well blended. Pour the dressing over the salad and toss. Arrange the salad on six serving plates and sprinkle each salad generously with the chopped hazelnuts.

Soft Shell Crabs with Orange Rice Salad

The citrus and olive flavors of the rice salad team well with sautéed seafood, as does a lighter style stainless-steel fermented and aged Chardonnay. If soft-shell crabs are not available substitute sautéed or grilled fish filets.

Serves 4

8 soft-shelled crabs
Flour

Salt and pepper, to taste
3 tablespoons butter or margarine

Dredge the crabs lightly in flour and sprinkle them with salt and pepper. Heat the butter in a large skillet over medium high heat. Add the crabs and sauté for 4 to 5 minutes per side, depending on the size of the crabs.

Orange Rice Salad

¼ cup orange juice
2 tablespoons lime juice
2 tablespoons chopped cilantro
½ tablespoon white wine vinegar
¼ teaspoon pepper
6 ounces rinsed, drained black beans

2 cups cooked rice
⅓ cup pimento stuffed olives, sliced
⅓ cup chopped red pepper
1 avocado, peeled and diced
½ large Valencia orange, peeled and diced
Lettuce leaves, for garnish

In a 1-cup measuring cup, combine the orange juice, lime juice, cilantro, wine vinegar, and pepper. Stir and set aside.

Combine the remaining ingredients in a mixing bowl and toss gently to mix. Pour the dressing over the salad and gently toss. Refrigerate for 4 hours before serving to allow flavors to meld. Serve the salad on lettuce leaves.

Tomato, Cheese, and Onion Pie

Vidalia onions from Georgia and fully ripe summer tomatoes make this dish a delightful light summer meal. Serve with some fresh steamed asparagus, a tossed salad, and a glass of stainless-steel fermented Chardonnay.

Serves 6

Pastry

1 ¼ cups flour
5 tablespoons butter
2 tablespoons vegetable shortening

4 to 5 tablespoons ice water
1 egg yolk
1 teaspoon Worcestershire sauce

Place the flour into the bowl of a food processor. Add the butter and shortening and process until the mixture resembles coarse meal. With the motor running add the ice water 1 tablespoon at a time. Process just until the dough forms a ball. (If necessary add 1 or 2 tablespoons more ice water.)

Place the dough on a floured surface and roll it out to fit a 10-inch deep dish pie plate. Line the pie plate with the dough and refrigerate for 30 minutes. Then line the pan with aluminum foil, shiny side down, weight it with beans or pie weights and bake the pie shell in a preheated 425° F. oven for 10 minutes. Carefully remove the pie weights and the aluminum foil. Beat together the egg yolk and Worcestershire sauce and light brush the mixture over the bottom of the pie crust. Bake for another 5 minutes. Cool the crust slightly while preparing the filling. Reduce the oven heat to 375° F.

Filling

3 tablespoons butter	2 large tomatoes
2 large Vidalia onions, sliced	3 eggs
½ pound Gruyère cheese	¾ cup whipping cream
2 tablespoons flour	

Melt the butter in a large frying pan; add the onions and sauté over medium heat until they turn golden, stirring frequently. This will take about 20 minutes.

Grate the cheese and toss it with the flour.

To assemble the pie, sprinkle a large handful of the cheese mixture over the pie crust. Spread the onions on top. Slice the tomatoes and arrange the slices over the onions. Sprinkle with the remaining cheese. Beat the eggs with the cream and pour the mixture over the pie. Bake in a preheated 375° F, oven for 40 minutes, or until the top is golden brown and the pie is firm in the middle.

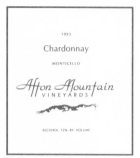

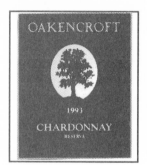

Oaked Chardonnay

Cheese Wafers

Pass these tangy Cheddar cheese wafers at a cocktail party. They pair well with an oaked Chardonnay.

Makes 4 dozen

1 ¼ cups all purpose flour
⅓ cup margarine of vegetable shortening
4 ounces grated Cheddar cheese
1 teaspoon caraway seeds

½ teaspoon salt
3 tablespoons cold water
Additional salt

Place all ingredients except the water in the bowl of a food processor and pulse until the shortening and cheese are cut into the flour, about 20 seconds. Add the water all at once through the food chute with the food processor running. Process about 10 seconds until a ball of dough is formed. (A little more water may have to be added, depending on the humidity of the day.)

Press the dough into a ball and then roll it out into a 15 by 12-inch rectangle on a floured board. Sprinkle lightly with salt. Cut into 1 ½-inch squares. Place the squares on an ungreased cookie sheet and bake in a preheated 400° F. oven for 8 to 10 minutes or until lightly browned.

Artichoke Frittata

The tangy combination of sharp Cheddar cheese and marinated artichoke hearts pairs well with an oaked Chardonnay.

Makes 16 pieces

3 (6 ounces) jars marinated artichoke hearts, drained and finely chopped
8 ounces sharp Cheddar cheese, grated
4 eggs, lightly beaten

6 single soda crackers, finely crushed
1 medium onion, finely chopped
Dash of Tabasco sauce
Salt and pepper, to taste

Combine all of the frittata ingredients in a bowl and then pour the mixture into a buttered 8-inch square baking pan. Bake in a preheated 325° F. oven for 50 minutes to 1 hour or until set. Cut into 1-inch squares and serve.

Hot Crabmeat in Pastry Shells

Water chestnuts combine with crabmeat and black olives in this first course dish. It may also be served as a luncheon entrée. Although water chestnuts are primarily cultivated in China, Japan, and the East Indies, the plant has also grown profusely in the Potomac River, where at one time it was reputed to be so dense that it stopped river traffic.

Serves 6

6 frozen puff pastry shells
1 pound crabmeat
2 cups coarsely chopped celery
1 can (8 ounces) water chestnuts, drained
    and sliced
½ cup sliced pitted black olives
2 tablespoons chopped onion

4 tablespoons chopped green pepper
¾ cup mayonnaise
¾ cup sour cream
½ cup dry white wine
¼ teaspoon garlic powder
¼ cup slivered almonds, toasted

Bake the puff pastry shells according to package directions. If two ovens are available, the puff pastry shells and the crabmeat may be baked at the same time. Otherwise keep the pastry shells warm while preparing the filling.

In a 1 ½ quart casserole combine the crabmeat, celery, water chestnuts, olives, onion, and green pepper. In a small mixing bowl combine the mayonnaise, sour cream, wine, and garlic powder. Fold the mayonnaise into the crab mixture. Bake in a preheated 350° F. oven for 30 to 35 minutes or until bubbly.

Spoon the hot crabmeat into the puff pastry shells and sprinkle with almonds. Serve immediately.

HOLLERITH

Cuvée Monticello

1992 VIRGINIA CHARDONNAY

ALC. 13% BY VOL.

Vineyard Pâté

This easy-to-prepare Pâté may be served as an hors d'oeuvre at a cocktail party or as a first course at a dinner party. It can also be taken along for a picnic in the vineyard and enjoyed with wine tasting.

Serves 8 to 10

2 tablespoons olive oil
1 onion, chopped
¾ cup brandy
2 garlic cloves, chopped
½ teaspoon salt
½ teaspoon pepper
1 teaspoon thyme
¼ teaspoon sage

⅛ teaspoon nutmeg
¼ teaspoon allspice
¾ pound ground pork
½ pound ground veal
¼ pound ground ham
2 eggs
¾ cup chopped pistachios
8 to 10 thin slices of bacon

Heat the oil in a skillet over medium heat. Add the onions and sauté them until lightly golden. Remove the onions to a large bowl. Add the brandy to the skillet and simmer on low heat until reduced to ⅓ cup. Pour the brandy into the bowl with the onions and add the garlic, salt, pepper, thyme, sage, nutmeg, and allspice. Then add the meats and the eggs, which have been lightly beaten. Add the nuts and mix well.

Line an 8 ½-inch loaf pan with the bacon slices, arranging them crossways so that the ends will overhang the sides of the pan. Spoon the meat mixture into the pan, smoothing out the top. Fold the bacon ends over the meat.

Place the pan in a 13x9x2-inch pan and add enough water to come up 1 ½ inches on the loaf pan. Bake in a preheated 350° F. oven for 1 ½ hours or until the center of the pâté registers 180° degrees on a meat thermometer.

Remove the loaf pan from the water and pour off any liquid that might have accumulated on the pâté. Cover it with aluminum foil and place a smaller pan filled with heavy objects such as a brick on top. Chill the pâté overnight and then slice and serve with French bread and cornichons (small pickles).

Plated Chowder

This recipe is reminiscent of the famous Maine fish chowder. Instead of a soup, it is an entree that features potatoes, corn, and cod or halibut, both of which are caught off the East Coast. As in a chowder, bacon adds an additional flavor to this dish.

Serves 4

6 small red potatoes
2 leeks, washed and trimmed
2 tablespoons butter
2 tablespoons vegetable oil
2 slices bacon, finely diced
⅓ cup fresh or canned corn
2 pounds halibut or cod filet, skinned
     and cut into 4 pieces

6 tablespoons bottled clam juice
6 tablespoons white wine
½ cup whipping cream
Salt and pepper, to taste
2 tablespoons chopped parsley

Cut the potatoes into very thin slices and the leeks into medium-thick slices. Melt the butter and oil in a large skillet over medium heat. Add the potatoes and sauté until crisp and golden, about 8 minutes. Remove the potatoes to a platter and keep them warm. Discard any remaining fat from the skillet.

Then add the bacon to the skillet and cook it over medium heat until it begins to render some fat. Add the leeks and sauté with the bacon until lightly browned. Stir in the corn and set aside.

Arrange the fish pieces in a pie pan, tucking under the ends if necessary for even thickness. Mix together the clam juice and wine and spoon ¼ cup of the mixture over the fish. Place a buttered piece of wax pepper the size of the pan over the fish, buttered side down. Bake in a preheated 325° F. oven for 12 to 15 minutes or until the fish flakes easily when tested with a fork. Strain the broth.

Add the strained broth, the remaining clam juice mixture and the cream to the corn in the skillet. Bring to a boil and cook over medium heat for 2 to 3 minutes or until the sauce thickens slightly. Season to taste with salt and pepper. Serve the fish with the sauce and potatoes. Garnish with parsley.

Salmon with Dill Sauce

Dill and salmon have an affinity for each other as the dill masks some of the richness of the fish. Serve this salmon entrée with small boiled red potatoes and green beans. Since salmon is a very rich and fatty fish it pairs well with an oaked Chardonnay.

Serves 4

4 salmon steaks	½ lemon, thinly sliced
1 small onion, sliced	¾ cup dry white wine

Place the salmon steaks in a large skillet; cover with the onion and lemon slices. Add the wine and sufficient water to barely cover the fish. Cover the skillet and bring to a boil. Reduce heat and simmer for 10 minutes, or until the fish flakes easily with a fork.

In the meantime, prepare the dill sauce. When the salmon is done, remove it to 4 warm plates and top with the dill sauce.

Dill Sauce

3 tablespoons butter or margarine	¼ cup chopped fresh dill
1 ½ tablespoons all-purpose flour	1 egg yolk
2 teaspoons Dijon mustard	3 tablespoons lemon juice
1 ¼ cups milk	Salt and pepper, to taste

Melt the butter in a medium-size saucepan over medium-low heat. Stir in the flour and then the mustard. Gradually add the milk, stirring constantly. Cook until the sauce is smooth and then add the dill. Beat the egg yolk, stir a little of the hot sauce into it, then add the egg mixture to the dill sauce. Blend in the lemon juice and season to taste with salt and pepper.

Tortellini with Scallops and Shrimp

This simple dish of scallops and shrimp in a cream sauce enriched with a little garlic and parsley emphasizes the delicate flavors of the seafood. It is served with tortellini for an interesting texture.

Serve 6 to 8

8 ounces scallops
8 ounces medium-sized shrimp
1 pound tortellini
8 tablespoons (1 stick) butter
2 cloves garlic, finely chopped

1 cup whipping cream
3 tablespoons chopped parsley
Salt and white pepper, to taste
Freshly grated Parmesan cheese

Wash the scallops in cold water and dry them well. Shell and devein the shrimp and wash and dry them.

Cook the tortellini in boiling salted water until they are tender but firm to the bite. Drain and keep the tortellini warm.

While the tortellini are cooking, melt the butter in a large skillet. When the butter foams, add the scallops, shrimp, and garlic. Cook for about 4 minutes over medium heat until seafood is barely done, stirring occasionally. Stir in the cream, parsley and salt and pepper. Cook 1 minute longer or until cream begins to thicken. Add the tortellini to the sauce and toss over low heat until the sauce coats the pasta, 20 to 30 seconds. Serve immediately with grated Parmesan cheese.

Penne with Sausages

Penne, the long tubular pasta, absorbs sauces well. A full-bodied oaked Chardonnay complements the spices and cream sauce. This dish may be prepared early in the day or one day ahead, refrigerated, and baked just before serving. If refrigerated bring the casserole to room temperature before baking.

Serves 4

3 medium zucchini, trimmed and
    cut in quarters lengthwise
1 tablespoon olive oil
2 mild Italian sausages, casings removed
2 hot Italian sausages, casings removed
1 medium onion, chopped
1 cup sliced fresh mushrooms

⅓ cup chopped red pepper
Salt and pepper, to taste
1 cup whipping cream
1 teaspoon dried oregano, crumbled
½ pound Fontina cheese, grated
¾ pound penne or other tubular pasta

Lightly grease or spray with non-stick cooking spray a 3 quart casserole or a large gratin dish. Cut each zucchini quarter in 1 ½-inch pieces.

Heat the oil in a large skillet over medium heat. Add the sausage, breaking it up with a fork or spoons and cook until no longer pink. Remove the sausage with a slotted spoon and discard all but 2 tablespoons of oil. Add the onion, mushrooms, and red peppers. Cook stirring occasionally until the vegetables begin to soften, about 5 minutes. Add the zucchini. Season with salt and pepper and continue to saute for another 5 minutes. Return the sausage to the skillet and add the cream and oregano and bring to a boil. Add half of the Fontina cheese to the sauce and stir until just melted.

In the meantime, cook the pasta in a large pot of boiling water until the pasta is al dente but still firm to the bite. Return the pasta to the pot and add the sauce. (If skillet is large enough add the pasta to it.) Transfer the mixture to the casserole. Top with the remaining cheese. Bake in a preheated 375° F. oven for 15 minutes or until heated through.

  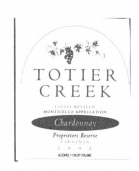

Veal with Caper-Mustard Sauce

This recipe originated in Germany, where the term pasta refers mainly to noodles, in this case the bow-tie type. An oaked Chardonnay pairs well with the piquant cream sauce.

Serves 2

5 ounces bow-tie noodles
Salt
2 tablespoons oil
1 tablespoon butter or margarine
8 ounces veal fillet, cut in ribbon strips
1 medium onion, chopped
3 ounces cremini (brown) mushrooms, sliced
2 ounces shiitake mushrooms, sliced

4 cornichons, cut in ribbon-like strips
⅔ cup chicken broth
¾ cup whipping cream
2 tablespoons capers, drained reserve liquid
1 tablespoon Dijon mustard
Cayenne pepper, to taste
¼ chopped fresh dill

Cook the noodles in lightly salted water according to package directions. Drain them and mix them with 1 tablespoon of the oil.

While the noodles are cooking prepare the sauce. Melt the butter and remaining oil in a large skillet over medium high heat. Add the veal strips and brown them quickly. Remove the veal; add the onions and mushrooms and sauté until all of the juice has evaporated. Then add the cornichons along with the chicken broth. Continue cooking until slightly reduced. Add the whipping cream, 1 tablespoon of the caper liquid, and the mustard and mix well. Season with salt and cayenne pepper, to taste. Reduce the liquid until the sauce is creamy, stirring occasionally. Then add the capers, dill, and veal strips. Heat through and serve over the bow-tie noodles.

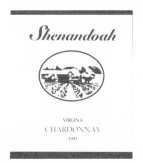

Chenin Blanc

Chenin Blanc is produced throughout the world and is generally finished in an off-dry-to sweet style. Its modern-times origin was around Anjou in the Loire Valley of France, where it has been grown for over 500 years. Vouvre is one of the most famous of the French Chenin Blancs from the Loire Valley. In recent years South Africa and California have become well-known for their Chenin Blancs.

The Chenin Blanc grape yields a fresh fruity wine with undertones of melons, pears, and peaches. It is particularly enjoyable with light food during hot summer months and is usually consumed young. A few vintners, particularly in California, are currently producing a dry Chenin Blanc which they age in oak to give it more complexity. Some vintners blend a modest amount of Chardonnay or Sauvignon Blanc with Chenin Blanc to soften its typically-high acidity. The large-volume wine producers in California use Chenin Blanc grown in the hot, inland valleys of California as a major element in their less-expensive bulk wines.

In Virginia, Afton Mountain Vineyards is the only grower and producer of Chenin Blanc wine. Shinko Corpora, the winemaker at Afton, gives her Chenin Blanc an off-dry finish.

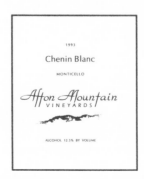

Watermelon Soup

Simple to prepare, this soup is a most unusual refreshing start to an informal meal. Chenin Blanc complements the fruitiness of the soup.

Serves 10

1 medium elongated watermelon
1 ½ cups buttermilk

2 tablespoons chopped fresh mint leaves
Mint leaves, for garnish

Cut the top third off the watermelon and take the pulp out of both sections. Eliminate the seeds and puree enough of the pulp in a food processor to yield 9 cups of fairly thick liquid. Add the buttermilk and chopped mint. Refrigerate the soup to thoroughly chill it.

Cut zigzags in the top of the larger piece of scooped-out watermelon shell. Refrigerate until ready to serve.

To serve, pour the soup into the cold watermelon shell and garnish with mint leaves. Serve in soup mugs.

Spinach Asparagus Salad

Strawberries and orange juice are the basis of this salad dressing which pairs well with Chenin Blanc. The dressing may also be used with various lettuces.

Serves 4

1 cup strawberries, stemmed
½ cup orange juice
2 tablespoons raspberry vinegar
2 tablespoons extra virgin olive oil
4 teaspoons honey

¼ teaspoon salt
8 cups trimmed spinach leaves
1 pound small asparagus spears, blanched
    and drained
4 tablespoon toasted slivered almonds

Combine the strawberries, orange juice, vinegar, olive oil, honey, and salt in the bowl of a food processor. Pulse on and off until the dressing is mixed, but still slightly chunky. Pour the dressing into a container, cover, and refrigerate.

To serve, place 2 cups of spinach on each of four plates. Top each with one-fourth of the asparagus and drizzle with about ⅓ cup dressing. Sprinkle each serving with 1 tablespoon of almonds.

Delaware

A naturally-created American hybrid, the Delaware was commercialized by a hybridizer in New Jersey around 1849. The pink Delaware grape became famous as the basis of sparkling wine produced near Delaware, Ohio—from which the grape derived its name. The Delaware American hybrid's early acceptance was due to the near absence of the "foxy" character of its Vitis Lubrusca *American parent. While having native American heritage, the vines are susceptable to phylloxera and fungus, although they are winter hardy.*

White wine made from the pinkish Delaware grape exhibits a delicate fruity, slightly spicy flavor. The grape produces high acidity and sugar levels, making Delaware particularly attractive for sparkling wines. For reasons lost in history, it is the most popular wine and table grape grown in Japan—perhaps because its delicate character as a wine is somewhat similar to that of sake, the traditional rice wine of Japan.

The only grower of the Delaware grape in Virginia is Archie Smith III at Meredyth Vineyards near Middleburg in northern Virginia. Archie says that the grapes usually have very high sugar content at harvest, so he ferments them into a sweet wine, typically with around 5 percent residual sugar. He has found that the pineapple flavors in the grape complement the sweetness to yield a balanced wine.

Pineapple Chicken

Pineapple, peppers, and ginger add an oriental flavor to this easy-to-prepare chicken dish. Its pineapple flavor is further enhanced by Delaware varietal wine.

Serves 4

1 (3 to 3 ½ pound) fryer, quartered
1 cup fresh pineapple chunks (2-inch pieces)
¾ cup green pepper chunks (2-inch pieces)
¾ cup red pepper chunks (2-inch pieces)
5 large mushrooms, thickly sliced
1 medium onion, thickly sliced

1 tablespoon low sodium soy sauce
½ teaspoon onion powder
½ teaspoon ground ginger
Salt and pepper, to taste
⅔ cup dry white wine, at room temperature

Place chicken in a large flat 13 x 9-inch baking dish. Add the pineapple, green and red peppers, mushrooms, and onion, being careful not to cover the chicken pieces with the vegetables. Drizzle the soy sauce over the chicken pieces. Sprinkle chicken with the onion powder, ground ginger, and salt and pepper, to taste.

Bake the chicken in a 375° F. oven for 30 minutes. Remove from oven and spoon the wine over the chicken pieces. (Wine should be at room temperature, so as not to crack the casserole dish) Return the chicken to the oven and bake for another 30 minutes, or until done. If a crisper skin is desired, turn on the top or broiler heat for a minute or two. To serve, cut the chicken in serving pieces, garnish with the vegetables and serve with steamed rice.

Pecan Pie

Although pecans are not grown in Virginia, Pecan Pie is a culinary tradition of the state. The richness of this moderately-sweet filling is due to the use of some brown sugar.

Serves 6 to 8

4 tablespoons butter or margarine, at room
   temperature
¼ cup sugar
¼ cup light brown sugar

1 cup light corn syrup
3 eggs
1 ½ cups pecan halves
Pastry for 9-inch pie (recipe follows)

Cream the butter and the sugars in a bowl until light and fluffy. Add the syrup and beat well. Then add the eggs, one at a time, beating well after each addition. Fold in the pecans.

Pour the filling into the prepared pie shell and bake in a preheated 350° F. oven for 50 minutes, or until a knife inserted halfway between the center and the outside of the filling comes out clean.

Pastry

1 cup all-purpose flour
3 tablespoons butter or margarine

3 tablespoons solid vegetable shortening
3 to 4 tablespoons ice water

Place the flour in a bowl. With a pastry blender cut in the butter and shortening until the solids are the size of very small peas. Fluff the mixture with a fork. Add the ice water, one tablespoon at a time, tossing the mixture with the fork until the dough sticks together and can be formed into a ball. Wrap the dough in plastic wrap and place in the refrigerator for at least one hour.

Remove dough from the refrigerator, place on a floured board, and roll 1 inch larger in diameter than the top surface of the pie pan. Place dough in pie pan; crimp the edges.

Gewürztraminer

Although almost universally associated with the French province of Alsace, Gewürztraminer is believed to be of Italian origin. The white Traminer grape first appears in historical literature as being grown in Termeno, in the Italian Tyrol, around 1,000 A.D. It has been popular in the Rhineland-Palatinate region of Germany for over 150 years. Gewürztraminer (or spicy Traminer) is a uniquely full-flavored strain of the Traminer variety. This particular strain is so valued in Alsace that it has become illegal to plant or refer to any other strain of the Traminer grape.

While the wine community terms Gewürztraminer as the Traminer with the spicy aroma, the aroma has no resemblance to that of spices. Rather it is more accurately described as that of tropical fruit or highly perfumed flowers, including lychees and roses. Some creative wine writers describe the aroma as facial cream-like. The Italian term for Gewürztraminer is Traminer Aromatico.

While Traminer is basically a white grape, the Gewürztraminer strain has a peachy glow. Gewürztraminer can be grown in hot summer climates. It attains its best fruity characteristics, however, in regions of moderate summer temperatures. Gewürztraminer is a difficult grape to grow, being susceptable to various diseases. Since the vines leaf early, they can be hurt by spring frost. The grape tends to be low in acid and must be picked at just the proper point of ripeness when acid, fruitiness, and sugar are in balance.

There are six wineries producing Gewürztraminer wine in Virginia: Afton Mountain Vineyards, Barboursville Vineyards, Oasis Vineyard, Prince Michel Vineyards, Rebec Vineyards, and Shenandoah Vineyards. Shinko Corpora at Afton Mountain produces an off-dry Gewürztraminer, as does Luca Paschina, winemaker and general manager at Barboursville. Luca bottles his Gewürztraminer under the Italian name for the varietal, Traminer Aromatico. He cold ferments the wine to retain as much of the fruity flavor as possible. Prince Michel, under the Rapidan River label, also uses cold fermenting but finishes it dry to provide a fruity, crisp wine.

Richard Hanson at Rebec prefers to finish his Gewürztraminer as a dessert wine by retaining approximately 5 percent sugar. Dirgham Salahi, co-owner and winemaker at Oasis, also produces a dessert wine from Gewürztraminer, which he calls Nector of Traminer. Shenandoah makes a small amount of Gewürztraminer which is finished off-dry and is sold only at the winery.

Chicken with Artichokes

The herbaceous flavor of artichokes in this chicken dish is enhanced by the fruitiness of a Gewürztraminer varietal wine.

Serves 4

1 (3 to 3 ½ pound) chicken, cut into
   serving pieces
2 tablespoons butter
1 tablespoon vegetable oil
12 small white boiling onions, skinned
1 (10 ounce) package frozen artichoke hearts,
   defrosted and drained

1 teaspoon lemon juice
½ cup dry white wine
½ cup chicken broth
Salt and pepper, to taste
¼ teaspoon dried thyme
1 bay leaf, broken in small pieces

Note: If desired, the chicken pieces may be skinned.

Heat the butter and oil in a 10 to 12-inch skillet over medium high heat and brown the chicken pieces. Remove the chicken from the skillet and place in a baking dish (13 x 9-inch or similar size).

In the same skillet, sauté the onions until golden brown. Place the onions in the dish with the chicken. Add the lemon juice to the skillet and sauté the artichoke hearts lightly. Arrange them in the baking dish with the chicken and onions. Combine the wine, chicken broth, salt, pepper, thyme and bay leaf. Pour this mixture over the chicken. Bake uncovered in a preheated 350° F. oven for 50 minutes to 1 hour, or until the chicken is done.

Chinese Spareribs

Gewürztraminer pairs well with Chinese dishes that have some sweet and salty characteristics. The fruity components of the wine complement the ginger and orange marmalade used in these Chinese Spareribs.

Serves 2 to 3

1 side pork spareribs
½ teaspoon pepper
½ cup light soy sauce
½ cup water

¼ cup finely minced fresh ginger
1 teaspoon garlic powder
1 cup orange marmalade

Cut the side of spareribs into 2-rib pieces and place them into an oblong baking dish. Sprinkle the ribs with the pepper. Bake in a preheated 350° F. oven for 1 hour. Pour off the fat.

Combine the soy sauce, water, ginger, garlic powder, and orange marmalade in a small bowl. Baste the spareribs with the sauce. Continue to bake the ribs basting them every 15 minutes three more times for a total cooking time of 2 hours.

Note: If finishing the ribs on a grill, bake them in the oven for 1 hour as directed above, then grill them over medium hot coals for 45 minutes, basing them 3 times.

Shenandoah

VIRGINIA
GEWÜRZTRAMINER
1993

BARBOURSVILLE
VINEYARDS
VIRGINIA

TRAMINER AROMATICO
MONTICELLO
1993
ESTATE BOTTLED

RAPIDAN RIVER

VIRGINIA
GEWÜRZTRAMINER
1992
PRODUCED AND BOTTLED BY VAVIN, INC., LEON, VIRGINIA
ALC 11% BY VOL

Ginger Pear Cake

The subtle fruit flavor and slight sharpness of ginger in this pear cake pairs well with a semi-sweet Gewürztraminer.

Serves 8

3 cups water
⅔ cup sugar
1 tablespoon lemon juice
3 large, uniform firm pears, peeled,
    halved, and cored
½ cup blanched almonds

¼ cup flour
1 teaspoon baking powder
1 teaspoon ground ginger
2 large eggs
⅔ cup sugar
5 tablespoons butter or margarine, melted

In a pan large enough to hold the pear halves in a single layer, combine the water, ⅔ cup sugar, and lemon juice. Bring to a boil, stirring until the sugar dissolves. Add the pear halves and simmer, uncovered, for 8 to 10 minutes or until the pears are tender. Remove the pears with a slotted spoon and place cut side down on paper towels to drain.

Butter a 9-inch round glass or ceramic baking dish. Place the pears in the dish with their cut sides down and stem end pointing to the center. Set aside while preparing the batter.

Chop the almonds with the flour, baking powder, and ginger in the bowl of a food processor until finely ground, about 1 to 2 minutes. Remove from the processor and set aside. Then put the eggs and remaining sugar in the bowl and process for 1 minute. With the machine running, add the butter and process for 10 seconds. Scrape down the sides of the bowl. Add the flour mixture and process just until the flour disappears. Pour the batter over the pears. Bake in a preheated 325° F. oven for 40 to 45 minutes or until a cake tester inserted in the center comes out clean.

Malvasia

One of the world's most ancient vines, Malvasia originated in Asia Minor and took its name from the Greek port of Monemvasia. Today this white wine grape is grown in Italy, Spain, and other countries surrounding the Mediteranean, as well as in California. Over the centuries a large number of different strains of Malvasia have evolved. In Italy alone, ten different strains are being cultivated.

Malvasia wine is vinified in a variety of styles; most, however, tend to be on the sweet side in order to moderate the strong perfumy character of the wine.

In Virginia, Barboursville Vineyards is the only grower and producer of Malvasia. Luca Paschina at Barboursville produces Malvasia (he spells it Malvaxia, based on the old Roman spelling) in a dessert-wine style and has bottled it in a striking thin bottle that is a replica of an Italian bottle found in the ruins of Barboursville in 1984.

Little Custards with Poached Nectarines and Hazelnut Cookies

The custard is sweetened with honey and flavored with chopped ginger, a pleasing contrast to the slight tartness of the stewed nectarines. Peaches may be substituted for the nectarines. Serve with Hazelnut Cookies and a semi-sweet dessert wine, such as Malvasia.

Serves 6

2 ¼ cups milk
1 teaspoon vanilla extract
4 slices (¼ inch thick) of fresh ginger

3 whole eggs
1 egg yolk
⅓ cup mild honey

Preheat the oven to 325° F.. Butter 6 custard cups. Place a baking pan large enough to hold the cups in the oven and fill with about 1 inch of hot water.

Put the milk in a medium-sized saucepan, add the vanilla and ginger, and scald. Beat the eggs together just to mix and stir in the honey. Slowly whisk the hot milk into the egg mixture. Strain the custard mixture through a sieve into a pitcher and fill the custard cups. Place the cups in the baking pan and bake in the preheated 325° F. oven for 45 minutes. The custard is set when a knife inserted into the center comes out clean. Cool on a rack. Cover custards and chill in the refrigerator until serving time.

Poached Nectarines

1 cup dry white wine
1 ½ cups water
Juice of half a lemon

¼ cup honey
6 nectarines, peeled and sliced.
Zest of half an orange, cut into julienne strips

Combine the wine, water, lemon juice and honey in a large skillet or sauté pan, and bring to a boil. Add the nectarine slices and poach gently until they are soft, about 3 to 4 minutes. With a slotted spoon remove the slices to a bowl. Add the orange zest to the poaching liquid and reduce the liquid over high heat until 1 cup remains. Set aside to cool. When cool the poaching liquid may be combined with the nectarines and placed in the refrigerator until served.

To assemble, cut around the edges of the custards and unmold on individual serving plates. Arrange the nectarine slices around the custards, and spoon the poaching syrup and zest over the top. Serve with Hazelnut Cookies.

Hazelnut Cookies

Makes about 4 dozen cookies

1 ½ cups flour
½ teaspoon baking powder
½ cup soft butter or margarine
1 scant cup sugar

1 egg
2 teaspoons vanilla extract
1 cup toasted hazelnuts, skinned and
    coarsely ground

In a bowl combine the flour and baking powder. In another bowl, cream the butter with the sugar. The add the egg and vanilla. Gradually add the flour mixture and the nuts, mixing well. Turn the dough onto a large piece of waxed paper and shape into a roll 2 inches in diameter. Chill the dough for several hours or overnight.

Slice dough ⅜-inch thick and place on ungreased cookie sheet. Slice only the amount of dough needed for one baking and return the rest to the refrigerator. Bake cookies in a preheated 375° F. oven for about 10 minutes or until golden brown. Remove the cookies to a rack and let them cool.

Upside Down Apple Tart

Apples have been a favorite fruit in Virginia since the first settlers brought apple seedlings for planting with them. Today Virginia is one of the largest producers of apples in the country. Ground almonds add crunchiness to the tart dough.

Serves 8

8 tablespoons (1 stick) butter or margarine
1 ¼ cups all-purpose flour
2 teaspoons sugar

½ cup ground almonds
1 egg yolk
3 tablespoons ice water

Cut the butter into the flour in a bowl until the mixture resembles fine crumbs. Stir in the almonds and sugar. Combine the egg yolk and water and slowly stir into the flour mixture with a fork. Stir well to combine. Then, using your hands, shape the dough into a ball. Place the dough between two large sheets of plastic wrap and, with a rolling pin, roll the dough 1 inch larger than a 9-inch round cake pan. Carefully place the dough in the refrigerator to chill for 20 minutes, while preparing the apples.

Apple Topping

3 tablespoons butter or margarine
¼ cup sugar
5 large tart apples such as Granny Smith,
    peeled, cored and sliced very thin

½ teaspoon cinnamon
½ teaspoon nutmeg
Whipped cream, for garnish

Place the butter and sugar in a 9-inch round cake pan and melt the mixture over low heat. Continue cooking, stirring constantly with a wooden spoon, until the mixture is a light golden brown. Remove from heat, cool slightly, and add the apple slices, making sure that the top is reasonably flat. Sprinkle the apples with the cinnamon and nutmeg.

Unwrap the pastry and fit it over the apples, tucking the edges under the crust. Bake in a preheated 400° F. oven for 30 to 35 minutes, or until the crust is lightly browned.

After removing the tart from the oven, immediately turn it upside down on a serving plate. Leave the pan on the tart for a few minutes to let all of the juice permeate the crust. Serve warm or cool with whipped cream, if desired.

Tart de Santiago

This tart, which is based on almonds, is one of the specialties of Santiago in northern Spain. Almonds are one of the prime agricultural products of that country. Both almond paste and marzipan are available in supermarkets. The marzipan is preferable because it is lighter in texture. Serve the tart with a glass of Malvasia.

Serves 10 to 12

Crust

1 ½ cups flour
1 tablespoon sugar
10 tablespoons butter or margarine

1 egg yolk
3 tablespoons ice water

Combine the flour and sugar in a bowl. Cut the butter into small pieces and then cut it into the flour until the mixture resembles coarse bread crumbs. Mix the egg yolk with the water and add it to the flour mixture, a tablespoon at a time. A little more water may be needed to work the dough into a ball. Sprinkle a little flour onto a pastry board and quickly, but gently, knead the dough four or five times to distribute the butter. Wrap the dough in plastic wrap and refrigerate it for at least one hour.

Roll the dough on a floured board to fit a 10-inch tart pan allowing, for a 1/2-inch overhang. Press the dough into the tart pan and fold the overhang back under the dough, pressing it into the side of the pan to form a fluted edge. Prick the bottom of the tart and bake in a preheated 375° F. oven for 12 minutes. Remove the tart pan from the oven and allow it to cool slightly while preparing the filling.

Filling

3 ½ ounces marzipan
9 tablespoons butter or margarine, softened
½ cup sugar
4 eggs, separated

7 tablespoons Amaretto
7 ounces almonds, ground
1 cup slivered almonds

Place the marzipan, butter, and sugar in a bowl and with an electric mixer beat the mixture at low speed until well combined. Then beat in 1 egg yolk at a time and the Armaretto. Fold in the almonds. Beat the egg whites until stiff and gently fold them into the batter.

Pour the batter into the partially baked tart shell and smooth the top. Sprinkle the slivered almonds on top of the filling. Bake in a 375° F. oven for 30 to 35 minutes or until a cake tester inserted in the center comes out clean. After 20 minutes of baking, lightly cover the top of the tart with aluminum foil to prevent the almonds from getting too brown.

Pound Cake

Pound cakes have been popular in Virginia since colonial days, when a slice of pound cake was offered to afternoon visitors. Originally a pound cake consisted of a pound each of flour, sugar, butter, and eggs. Modern recipes have evolved with better proportions. This cake is lightened by aerating the dry ingredients and then adding butter and liquids. The use of cake flour also contributes to the lightness of the cake.

Serves 8 to 10

1 ½ cups cake flour, sifted
¾ cup sugar
1 teaspoon baking powder
3 tablespoons milk

3 large eggs
1 teaspoon vanilla extract
13 tablespoons butter or margarine, softened

Grease and flour an 8x4x2 ½-inch loaf pan. In a large bowl combine the flour, sugar, and baking powder. With an electric mixer at low speed mix these dry ingredients for about

1 minute. Combine the milk, eggs, and vanilla in another bowl. Add the butter and half of the egg mixture to the dry ingredients, mixing at low speed until blended. Then beat at medium speed for 1 minute.

Add the remaining egg mixture in 2 batches, beating well after each addition. Pour the batter into the prepared pan and bake in a preheated 350° F. oven for 55 to 60 minutes or until a wooden toothpick or cake tester inserted in the center of the cake comes out clean. Cool the cake in the pan on a rack, then slice and serve.

Almond Biscotti

These twice baked Italian cookies are intensely crunchy and are perfect for dipping into a dessert wine. Toasted hazelnuts may be substituted for the almonds. Pair these Italian cookies with a glass of Malvasia.

Makes about 40 pieces

2 cups all-purpose flour
¾ cup sugar
1 teaspoon baking powder
2 large whole eggs
1 large egg yolk
1 teaspoon vanilla

2 tablespoons grated orange rind
1 ¾ cups skinned whole almonds, lightly
    toasted and coarsely chopped
Egg wash made by beating together 1 egg
    and 1 teaspoon water

In a bowl blend together the flour, sugar, and baking powder with an electric mixer at low speed. In another small bowl whisk together the whole eggs, egg yolk, vanilla and grated orange rind. Add the egg mixture to the flour and beat until a dough is formed. Stir in the nuts. The dough will be very stiff.

Turn the dough onto a lightly floured board, knead it several times and then divide it in half. Form each dough piece into a flat-like log about 12 inches by 2 inches. Place the logs 3 inches apart on a greased and floured baking sheet. Then brush them with the egg wash.

Bake the logs in a preheated 300° F. oven for 50 minutes. Then let them cool on the baking sheet on a rack for 10 minutes. Cut the logs into ½-inch thick slices on a cutting board and arrange them cut side down on the baking sheet. (This will take two baking sheets. Be sure to lightly grease and flour the second sheet.) Bake the slices in the 300° F. oven for 15 minutes on each side. Transfer the biscotti to racks to cool and store them in an airtight container.

Marsanne

Grown principally in the northern Rhône Valley of France, Marsanne is a vigorous producer. This white grape is also grown in Australia and Switzerland. Wine from the Marsanne grape is deep-colored with a tint of brown. The wine does not age well and is generally drunk while young. A number of traditional vintners in France still age their Marsanne in oak barrels, however.

Dennis Horton of Horton Vineyards in Orange County is the only grower and producer of Marsanne in Virginia, having planted 1.25 acres in 1991. Horton has the grapes hand picked and then chilled overnight. The next day the juice is given six hours of skin contact. Horton follows the traditional French method of fermenting and aging Marsanne in oak barrels to give it greater complexity. The wine receives six months of aging in the barrels before bottling, giving it just a hint of oak.

Vichyssoise

Vichyssoise is a leek and potato soup with a French name. It was created in America by Louis Diat while he was the Chef des Cuisine at the Ritz-Carlton in New York early in the nineteen hundreds. Since it was first being served for the opening of the roof garden at the Ritz on a hot summer's day, he decided to serve it cold. It has been served that way ever since. However, this version is equally delicious warm.

Serves 4

2 tablespoons butter
3 leeks, white part only, sliced
1 medium onion, chopped
1 medium white potato, cut into cubes
1 ½ cups water
1 ½ cups chicken broth

¾ cup whipping cream
Lemon juice to taste, about 1 tablespoon
Dash of white pepper
3 or 4 drops Tabasco sauce
Salt to taste
Chopped chives or lemon thyme, for garnish

Melt the butter in a medium-sized saucepan. Add the leeks and onion and cook very gently over medium-low heat for about 15 minutes or until the vegetables are wilted. Do not brown. Add the potatoes, water, and chicken broth. Bring to a boil and gently simmer, covered, until potato is tender, about 20 minutes.

Add the cream and simmer, uncovered another 5 minutes. Puree the mixture in a blender. Strain and rub through a sieve to ensure that there are no large pieces of vegetable in the soup. Add lemon juice, white pepper, Tabasco sauce, and salt to taste. Chill thoroughly. Serve garnished with chopped chives or lemon thyme leaves.

Monkfish Kebobs

Although a rather ugly fish, monkfish has often been called the "poor man's lobster" because of its firm flesh. It is ideal for grilling as in this recipe for kebobs.

Serves 4

⅔ cup olive oil
3 tablespoons lemon juice
1 tablespoon chopped fresh parsley
1 tablespoon chopped fresh basil
1 clove garlic, minced
¼ teaspoon salt

¼ teaspoon pepper
2 pounds monkfish
½ green pepper
½ red pepper
16 cherry tomatoes

Cut the monkfish and peppers into 1½-inch cubes. Combine the olive oil, lemon juice, basil, garlic, salt, and pepper in a shallow dish. Add the fish, cover, and marinade in the refrigerator for 5 hours or overnight.

Thread the fish alternately with the pepper pieces and tomatoes onto 8 water-soaked bamboo skewers. Grill 4 inches above hot coals for about 3 minutes on each side, brushing with the marinade occasionally. Serve with rice.

Scallops in Wine Sauce

Sea scallops are harvested off the coast of Virginia year-round and have been cooked by coastal residents since the first settlers arrived. Today, with rapid means of transportation, fresh scallops are available inland. This recipe combines sea scallops with vegetables in a creamy wine sauce. The dish is garnished with puff pastry and baked.

Serves 4

1 sheet puff pastry from 1 package (17 ¼ ounces) frozen puff pastry sheets
2 tablespoons butter or margarine
2 medium zucchini, thinly sliced
1 carrot, cut into 1-inch julienne strips
5 large mushrooms, sliced
¼ cup chopped red pepper
2 tablespoons flour

½ cup whipping cream
¼ cup milk
2 tablespoons freshly grated Parmesan cheese
¼ teaspoon dried thyme
⅛ teaspoon pepper
3 tablespoons dry white wine
1 egg white, beaten
Freshly grated Parmesan cheese, for garnish

Thaw the sheet of puff pastry and, with a glass or cookie cutter, cut it into 2-inch rounds. Refrigerate the puff pastry rounds while preparing the scallops.

Melt the butter in a large skillet over medium heat. Add the zucchini, carrots, mushrooms, and red pepper and sauté for 3 to 4 minutes, until the vegetables are crisp-tender. Sprinkle the flour over the vegetables and stir gently to combine. Add the cream and milk and cook for 1 minute, stirring constantly. The mixture will be very thick. Add the scallops, Parmesan cheese, thyme, and pepper and cook over medium heat until the mixture comes to a boil. Remove from heat and stir in the wine.

Spoon the scallop mixture into an ungreased, 9-inch quiche pan. Place circles of puff pastry around the edges of the dish, leaving the center exposed. Lightly brush each pastry circle with beaten egg white and sprinkle with some Parmesan cheese. Bake in a preheated 375° F. oven for 25 to 30 minutes, until the pastry is golden brown and the scallop mixture is bubbling.

Chicken Breasts with Three Mustard Sauce and Glazed Carrots

Three mustards are combined in a light cream sauce to serve with sautéed chicken breasts. Marsanne pairs well with the slightly sweet orange flavors of the sauce and the sweetness of the glazed carrots which are cooked in beef broth and beer.

Serves 4

2 whole large chicken breasts, skinned, boned, and split
Salt, pepper, and paprika
1 tablespoon olive oil
1 tablespoon butter

½ cup dry vermouth
½ tablespoon grainy mustard
1 tablespoon Dijon mustard
1 tablespoon honey-orange mustard
⅔ cup whipped cream

Sprinkle both sides of each chicken breast half with salt and pepper, and then sprinkle each side liberally with paprika.

Heat the olive oil and butter in a large skillet over medium heat. Sauté the chicken breasts until browned, about 4 minutes. Then turn and brown the other side, also for about 4 minutes. Remove the chicken pieces to a warm plate and cover them loosely with aluminum foil to keep them warm.

Add the vermouth to the skillet, scraping up any brown particles. Then whisk in the three mustards and the cream. Continue to cook the sauce until it is slightly thickened, about 3 minutes. Add more mustard, if desired. Return the chicken to the skillet and turn the pieces to coat them with the sauce. Serve at once.

Glazed Carrots

1 ½ pounds carrots
1 teaspoon grated lemon peel
¼ teaspoon pepper
1 tablespoon sugar

2 tablespoons butter, cut in pieces
1 cup beef broth
1 cup beer

Peel the carrots and cut them in half lengthwise. Then cut them into 2 to 3-inch pieces. Place the carrots in a large skillet and sprinkle them with the pepper and sugar. Then dot them with the butter. Add the beef broth and the beer. Bring to a boil, then reduce the heat and simmer the carrots, uncovered, for about 40 to 50 minutes, stirring occasionally. The liquid should be thick and syrupy and the carrots done. If necessary remove carrots with a slotted spoon when tender and continue boiling the liquid until syrupy. Return the carrots to the skillet and coat with the liquid, then serve.

Moscato (Muscat)

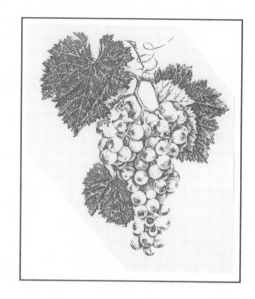

Many historians believe that Muscat is the oldest grape family known to man, having originated in the Near East. They believe that the modern Vitis Vinifera family of European wine grapes descended from this ancient species. Today, even within the Muscat variety, there are hundreds of strains of Muscat. A versatile grape that does best in warm climates, Muscat is grown for use as raisins and table grapes as well as wine. Of the many varieties of Muscat, the Muscat Blanc (also called Muscat de Frontignan in France and Moscato Bianca in Italy) is most commonly used for wine.

Muscat wines are typically styled as dessert wines, although in Italy Moscato is used as the basis of Italy's well-known sparkling wine, ASTI Spumante. Muscat is also used in Vermouth. Muscat grapes are especially rich in flavor but are low in acidity. Therefore, they must be picked early to achieve proper balance in the wine.

Within Virginia there are no producers offering Muscat at this writing. Both Steve Haskell at Villa Appalaccia on the Blue Ridge Parkway near Meadows of Dan and Luca Paschina at Barboursville Vineyards indicate they plan to introduce Muscat wine within the next year. Both expect to finish their Moscato in a semi-sweet style

Delicate Pancakes with Blueberry Sauce

In a different approach to a traditional brunch entreé, very thin pancakes are rolled like crepes and served with a fresh blueberry sauce. Similar to crêpes, these pancakes can also be served as a dessert. Accompany with a glass of Moscato.

Serves 4

Pancakes

1 cup all-purpose flour	2 eggs, slightly beaten
¼ teaspoon salt	1½ cups milk
1 teaspoon baking powder	1 teaspoon vanilla extract
1 teaspoon cornstarch	Butter for cooking

In a bowl mix together the flour, salt, baking powder, and cornstarch. Add the eggs, milk, and vanilla extract, blending all ingredients well. Do not overmix. Refrigerate the batter while preparing the Blueberry Sauce.

To cook the pancakes, heat an 8-inch nonstick sauté pan on medium heat. Melt approximately 1 tablespoon of butter and add about ⅛ cup of batter. Brown each side of the pancake, roll up and place on a warm platter. Continue cooking pancakes until all of the batter has been used. Serve with Blueberry Sauce.

Blueberry Sauce

½ cup semi-dry white wine	1 teaspoon cornstarch mixed with
1 orange, zested and juiced	1 teaspoon water
1 cinnamon stick	2 cups fresh or frozen blueberries

Bring the wine, orange zest and juice, and cinnamon stick to a boil. Turn heat to medium and cook for 1 minute. Add the cornstarch mixture and bring to a boil. When the mixture has thickened, add the blueberries and toss for 1 minute (longer if blueberries are frozen) until the berries are heated through. Serve over the pancakes.

Orange Chiffon Cake

This light chiffon cake may be served with fresh fruit and a glass of semi-sweet Moscato.

Serves 10 to 12

2 ¼ cups cake flour, sifted
1 cup sugar
1 tablespoon baking powder
½ cup vegetable oil
¾ cup frozen orange juice, concentrate, thawed

6 egg yolks
3 tablespoon grated orange zest
8 egg whites
½ teaspoon cream of tartar

Sift the flour, sugar, and baking powder together into a large bowl. Add the oil, orange juice, egg yolks, and orange zest. Beat with an electric mixer at medium speed until very smooth. Combine the egg whites and cream of tartar in another large bowl. Beat at high speed until stiff peaks form. Gradually and gently, fold the batter into the egg whites with a large spatula. Pour into an ungreased 10-inch tube pan and smooth out the top. Bake in a pre heated 325° F. oven for 55 minutes to 1 hour, or until a cake tester inserted in the center comes out clean.

Remove the cake from the oven and invert the pan immediately so that is rests on the center core only, with the remaining surfaces of the pan and cake free of the counter top. Allow the cake to hang until it is completely cool; then remove from the pan.

Niagara

This white American hybrid has been commercialized since the 1870s. It is sometimes referred to as the "white Concord" and continues to be popular as a table grape. Because of its rugged Vitis Labrusca parentage, wine from the Niagara exhibits an aggressive "foxiness." To hide this characteristic, Niagara is typically produced as a sweet wine. The sugar balances the strong flavor to yield a pleasant fruity wine.

The only grower and producer of Niagara varietal wine in Virginia is Chateau Morrisette on the Blue Ridge parkway south of Roanoke near Meadows of Dan. The wine maker at Chateau Morrisette, Robert Burgin, finishes his Niagara wine in the dessert wine style, maintaining a sugar content of approximately 5 percent. Chateau Morrisette bottles the wine under a Sweet Mountain Laurel label. Burgin also uses Niagara in two of his popular blended wines, Virginia Blush and Red Mountain Laurel.

Rhubarb-Strawberry Tart

Rhubard and Strawberries have an affinity for each other, as one is sweet and the other acidic. In this tart the fruit is topped with a light custard.

Serves 8

Crust

1 ¼ cupsflour
¼ cup sugar

½ cup (1 stick) butter, preferably unsalted
2 to 3 tablespoons ice water

Combine the flour and sugar. Cut the butter into small pieces and cut it into the flour until the mixture resembles fine crumbs. Sprinkle with the ice water, and with a fork form it into a ball. Depending on the humidity of the day, more water may be needed. Place the dough in the refrigerator for at least 1 hour.

Filling

1 ½ pounds rhubarb, trimmed and cut
    into 1-inch pieces
6 large strawberries, sliced
⅔ cup sugar

3 eggs separated
¼ cup whipping cream
Grated rind of ½ lemon

Place the rhubarb and strawberries in a bowl and sprinkle with half of the sugar. Let the mixture sit for 30 minutes to draw out the juice.

In the meantime, roll out the pastry and line a buttered 10 inch tart pan with it. Prick the pastry well and bake it blind (without pie weights) for 10 minutes in a preheated 375° F. oven.

Drain the rhubarb, reserving the juice, and place it in the pastry shell. Sprinkle the filling with half of the remaining sugar and return the tart to the oven to bake for 20 minutes.

Beat the egg yolks with the remaining sugar and beat in the rhubarb juice and the cream. Add the lemon rind. Beat the egg whites until stiff, but not dry, and fold them into the egg yolk mixture. Pour this custard over the rhubarb. Return the tart to the oven and bake for another 20 minutes. Serve warm or cold.

Dark Fruitcake

Fruitcakes have become traditional Thanksgiving and Christmas cakes. They are not original to America, but emigrated from England with the early colonists. The mixture of candied fruit in this traditional recipe may be varied to suit your fancy, just make sure it is 2 pounds in total weight, not including the raisins. A glass of Niagara and a slice of homemade fruitcake is an ideal way to extend holiday cheer.

Makes 1 ten-inch cake

½ pound candied citron
¼ pound candied lemon peel
¼ pound candied orange peel
½ pound candied cherries
½ pound candied pineapple
½ pound golden raisins
½ pound dark raisins
¼ pound currants
½ pound figs, cut in small pieces
⅔ cup brandy
¼ pound blanched, slivered almonds
¼ pound pecans, whole or large pieces

2 cups flour
½ teaspoon nutmeg
½ teaspoon cinnamon
¼ teaspoon ginger
⅛ teaspoon ground cloves
½ teaspoon baking soda
½ cup (1 stick) butter or margarine,
   at room temperature
¾ cup sugar
¾ cup brown sugar
5 eggs
3 tablespoons orange juice

The day before, combine the candied fruit, raisins, and figs in a bowl. Add the brandy, combining it well with the fruit. Cover the bowl and let sit overnight.

The following day grease a 10-inch tube pan and line it with brown paper. Add the nuts to the fruit and sift ½ cup of the flour over the mixture. Combine the remaining 1 ½ cups of flour with the spices and baking powder.

In another bowl cream the butter until soft, add the sugars, a little at a time, and cream until smooth. Stir in the eggs and orange juice. Then add the flour mixture and mix thoroughly. Pour the batter over the fruit and nuts and mix thoroughly. Place the cake batter in the pan and lightly press it down to make a compact cake. Bake in a preheated 275° F. oven for 3 ¼ hours or until a cake tester inserted in the center comes out clean.

Remove the cake from the oven, let it stand for half an hour and then turn out of pan. Peel off the brown paper and let the cake cool thoroughly. If desired the fruitcake may be wrapped in a brandy, rum, cognac, or sherry soaked cheese cloth. Place the cake in an airtight container and let the cake age for two to three weeks before serving. The cake may be stored without the cheesecloth in an airtight container and brushed every few days with brandy, rum, cognac or sherry. Do not over baste. The cake should be firm at the end of the aging period.

Pinot Grigio (Gris)

This mutation of Pinot Noir received its name from the blue-gray berries and the sometimes-pinkish juice contained in them. Grigio's traditional home is the central region of Europe, ranging from France to Italy in the south and east through Germany and Hungary to Russia. Pinot Gris plantings in Germany, where it is called Ruländer after the vineyardist who first commercialized the variety in 1711, exceed that in any other country. In the Alsace region of France, Pinot Gris is traditionally known as Tokay d'Alsace, having been imported there from Hungary in the 1750s.

Pinot Grigio wine yields a spicy aroma and usually has slightly below average acidity. Because of the low acid, vineyardists tend to harvest the grapes somewhat early which tends to lessen the fruitiness of the wine.

The two producers of Pinot Grigio in Virginia, both with Italian roots, are Gabrielle Rausse at Jefferson Vineyards and Luca Paschina at Barboursville Vineyards. Not surprisingly, both produce a dry Pinot Grigio in the Italian style. They give the juice extra time on the skins to develop character in this rather delicate wine. By fermenting the wine with a dry finish, it makes an excellent accompaniment to light foods.

Carrot Velvet Soup

This carrot soup is a delectable start to a dinner party. Ginger and curry powder give this soup a pleasing oriental flavor. The soup may be prepared several days in advance and simply reheated at serving time.

Serves 4

3 tablespoons butter or margarine
1 medium carrot, chopped
1 leek, white part only, chopped
3 tablespoon chopped fresh ginger
1 teaspoon Oriental (toasted) sesame oil
4 cups chicken broth

¾ cup dry white wine
1 ¼ pound carrots, peeled and cut in chunks
Curry powder, to taste
Salt and pepper, to taste
Chopped fresh parsley, for garnish

Melt the butter in a large saucepan. Add the chopped onion, leek, ginger and sesame oil and cook over low heat until onion and leeks are limp and transparent, about 15 minutes. Stir the mixture often. Add the chicken broth, wine, and carrots and continue to cook, covered, until the carrots are very soft, about 25 to 30 minutes. Puree the soup in batches in a food processor until very smooth and velvety. Return the soup to the saucepan and heat; then season with curry powder and salt and pepper, to taste. Ladle into individual soup bowls and garnish with parsley.

Red, White, and Green Pasta

The Red, White, and Green Pasta (the colors in Italy's flag) can be served hot as a first course, or cold at a picnic. Sprinkling lemon juice over the avocado slices prevents their discoloration and adds to the flavor of the dish. Serve the pasta with a glass of Pinot Grigio, a wine of Italian origin.

Serves 4

12 ounces fusilli (short twisted pasta)
1 avocado
2 tablespoons lemon juice
¼ teaspoon chili powder

4 tablespoons olive oil
2 plum tomatoes, peeled and chopped
2 tablespoons chopped parsley

Cook the pasta in boiling water until al dente.

In the meantime, peel and cut the avocado in slices. Then cut the slices in half again, making about 2-inch pieces. Place the avocado pieces in a bowl and sprinkle with lemon juice and chili powder.

Drain the pasta, place in a bowl, and add 3 tablespoons of the olive oil. Toss to combine. If serving warm, place the pasta in a warm oven, 150° F., for 5 minutes.

Just before serving add the avocado pieces, tomato, parsley, and remaining tablespoon of olive oil to the pasta. Toss to combine and serve immediately.

If serving cold, do not place the pasta in the oven, but combine all ingredients with the drained pasta.

Stuffed Chicken Breasts in Wine Sauce

Italian in origin, this simple-to-prepare dish makes an elegant company meal when accompanied by a Pinot Grigio.

Serves 8

4 whole chicken breasts
Seasoning salt
1 stick butter or margarine, at room
    temperature
½ teaspoon oregano
½ teaspoon marjoram

1 teaspoon chopped fresh parsley
¼ pound Monterey Jack cheese
1 cup flour
2 eggs beaten
1 cup dried bread crumbs
½ cup dry white wine

Split the chicken breasts in half. Skin and bone them and then pound them to about 1/8 inch thickness. Lightly sprinkle the chicken breasts with seasoned salt.

Whip the butter until fluffy and add the oregano, marjoram and parsley. Cut the cheese into 8 long pieces and spread them with half of the butter mixture. Place 1 stick of cheese on each chicken cutlet and roll it like a jelly roll, tucking the sides in.

Coat each piece of chicken with flour. Then dip it into the beaten egg and roll it in bread crumbs. Place the chicken pieces in a flat baking dish. (The chicken breasts may be prepared to this point early in the day and refrigerated until time to bake them.)

Bake chicken rolls, uncovered, in a preheated 350° F. oven (do not preheat oven, if refrigerated first) for 20 minutes. In the meantime, melt the remaining butter and stir in the wine. Pour the mixture over the chicken and continue baking for an additional 15 to 20 minutes. Serve with the pan juices and rice.

Riesling

A vine that does best in cooler northern climes, Riesling is grown and enjoyed throughout the world. The vine is a native of Germany, being a descendant of a Rhineland wild grape variety. Records show that the Germans first domesticated it in the ninth century. The first recorded significant wine was made from this grape in 1435 in what is today Russelsheim, outside of Frankfurt. By the mid-1500s, there were considerable plantings of Riesling along the Rhine and Mosel Rivers but the first vineyard devoted solely to Riesling dates from 1716 at Schloss Johannisberg in the Rheingau.

Except for Alsace, one of the few places Riesling cannot be grown is in France, and that is by law. French law states that Riesling cannot be grown any further inside of France than 30 miles from the German border. This area covers the region of Alsace along the western bank of the Rhine river. Many years ago the French decided to protect their own domestic white varietal grapes from a perceived German wine-grape invasion.

More than any other great grape variety, Riesling has suffered from corruption of its name, as it has been applied to many mediocre grape varieties. California has created its Grey and Emerald Riesling labels, and has popularized the name Johannisberg Riesling for a particular clone of Riesling popular in California. This was done for purely promotional reasons to capitalize on the famous wine-growing region around Johannisberg, a small area in Germany along the Rhine that has been recognized for outstanding Riesling. Other regions of the world followed suit by attaching a geographical name to their Riesling, such as Russian- and Romanian-named Rieslings. Even the Germans have been guilty of using the Riesling name for lesser grapes.

The vines of the Riesling bud late in the spring and the grapes ripen late in the fall, thereby reducing the possibility of bud damage from late spring frosts. In America it is being grown in the cooler regions of California, northeastern United States, and the hillsides of

Virginia. Riesling grapes manage to retain their high acidity through the long growing cycle and even after the normal harvesting period. This high acidity makes Riesling popular as a late-harvested sweet dessert wine.

Traditionally Riesling is made off-dry with a fruity finish. In recent years, a number of California wine makers have been subjecting their Rieslings to some oak aging. However, extensive oaking can quickly destroy the grape's unique fruity aroma. Riesling is a great sipping wine but it also goes well with pork or poultry dishes that have a somewhat sweet sauce. A semi-dry Riesling also goes well with slightly spicy foods as it provides a good contrast to mild spices. In addition, Riesling is a good companion to fruit desserts that do not contain cream. An off-dry Riesling also pairs well with vegetables, such as vegetable-based soups, and with slightly salty dishes, such as ham. A few vintners prefer to follow the Alsation style of Riesling by finishing it completely dry. This permits the wine to accompany heavier foods that can stand up to the more prominent acidity of the wine.

Riesling has become one of the favorite wines of Virginia. Currently half of the 42 vintners in Virginia grow and produce Riesling wine. With its warm humid summers, Virginia is about as far south as this grape can be grown in the eastern United States, while still producing a crisp fruity wine. Generally, Virginia vintners finish their Riesling in the traditional German off-dry style, which typically means approximately 1 percent sugar—thus retaining the delightful fruity character of the grape while moderating its high acidity. Richard Hanson at Rebec Vineyards prefers to finish his Riesling as a dessert wine, retaining roughly 5 percent residual sugar, as does Ken McCoy at Rose River. At the other end of the scale Jamie Lewis at Totier Creek Vineyards and Chris Johnson at Rapidan River (Prince Michel) are the only Virginia vintners offering a dry Riesling. Both wineries also bottle a traditional off-dry version.

Pea Soup à la Aschinger

This soup is a re-creation of the one served at Aschingers, the famous Berlin restaurant, which has been in existence for more than 150 years. The soup may be made with either green or yellow dried peas. A semi-sweet Riesling pairs well with the natural sweetness and saltiness of the ham used in the soup.

Serves 4 to 6

1 pound split peas, green (or yellow)
½ pound sliced medium lean bacon,
    cut into strips
1 large onion chopped
1 leek, white part only, sliced
1 ham bone with a little meat left on it,
    or 1 meaty ham hock

3 medium potatoes, diced
2 cups chicken broth
6 cups water
½ teaspoon dried basil
¼ teaspoon dried marjoram
Salt and pepper, to taste
½ cup plain croutons, optional

Soak the peas for an hour in water before cooking. Drain.

In a large heavy soup pot cook the bacon briskly until the fat has been rendered. Remove the bacon and drain the fat, reserving 2 tablespoons of it. Add the 2 tablespoons of fat back to the pot and add the onions and leek, cooking them over medium heat until they are limp.

Then add the peas, reserved bacon, ham bone, potatoes, chicken broth, water, basil, and marjoram to the soup pot. Cover and bring to a slow boil, then continue cooking over low heat for 45 to 60 minutes, stirring occasionally.

Remove the ham bone and detach any fragments of meat from it. Chop the meat into small pieces. If a smoother texture is desired puree half of the soup in a blender or use an immersion blender to slightly puree the soup in the pot. Add the ham pieces and season to taste with salt and pepper. Serve in soup bowls and garnish with croutons, if desired.

Peach Soup

There is nothing as refreshing on a warm day than a chilled soup. Simple to prepare, this soup can be made a day ahead of serving. Serve with a glass of chilled Riesling.

Serves 4 to 6

2 cups fresh peaches, peeled and sliced
1 tablespoon lemon juice
¼ to ⅓ cup sugar, depending on
    tartness of peaches

2 cups dry white wine
1 cup whipping cream
Fresh mint leaves, for garnish

Immediately after slicing peaches sprinkle them with the lemon juice. Place the peaches, sugar and wine in a medium-sized saucepan. Slowly bring mixture to a simmer and simmer for 6 to 8 minutes or until peaches start to soften. Add cream and continue to simmer slowly for another 10 minutes. Place mixture in a food processor and process until smooth. Chill. Garnish each serving with a mint leaf.

Baked Ham with Scalloped Potatoes

An apricot-brandy glaze adds additional flavor to ham that is baked with wine. Gruyère cheese and porcini mushrooms season scalloped potatoes in a dish that complements the ham. A semi-dry Riesling pairs well with the saltiness of the ham.

Serves 6 to 8

1 (6 to 7 pound) shank-half ham
¾ cup white wine
Ground cloves

⅔ cup apricot preserves
½ cup brandy

Place a piece of heavy-duty aluminum foil, which is large enough to encase the ham, in a large baking dish. Place the ham, fat and rind side up, on the foil and gradually pour the wine over it. Close the aluminum foil, wrapping the ham loosely. Bake in a preheated 325° F. oven for 20 minutes per pound.

A half hour before the end of the cooking time, combine the apricot preserves and the brandy in a small saucepan and warm the mixture over low heat. Remove the ham from the oven and discard the aluminum foil and any accumulated juices in the pan. Remove any rind from the ham and score the fat. Sprinkle the ham lightly with ground cloves and baste it with some of the apricot mixture. Return the ham to the oven and raise the temperature to 350° F. Bake ham another 30 minutes, basting several times with the apricot mixture. Slice the ham and serve with Scalloped Potatoes.

Scalloped Potatoes

½ ounce dried porcini mushrooms
3 tablespoons butter
6 ounces crimini mushrooms, sliced
6 ounces shiitake mushrooms, sliced
1 large onion, sliced

6 large Idaho baking potatoes
8 ounces Gruyère cheese, shredded
2 cups milk
1 cup whipping cream

Soak the porcini mushrooms in hot water until soft. Remove the mushrooms, squeeze them almost dry, and chop them coarsely. (Save the water for soup stocks.) Melt the butter in a large skillet over medium heat, add all of the mushrooms and the onion. Sauté until most of the mushroom liquid has evaporated.

In the meantime, peel the potatoes and slice them thinly. If they have to stand for a while place them in a dish of cold water.

Butter an ovenproof casserole and place a layer of potatoes on the bottom. Top with some of the mushroom mixture and some of the grated cheese. Continue making layers until all of the potatoes, mushrooms, and cheese are used, ending with cheese on top. Combine the milk and whipping cream and gently pour it over the potatoes so that the liquid barely reaches the top. If more liquid is needed, add it in equal amounts of milk and cream. Bake in a 375° F. oven for 1 hour or until the potatoes are done and the top is lightly browned.

110

Viennese Marble Cake

This cake was inspired by the abundance of apricots grown around Vienna. It keeps moist for several days. Serve with a glass of Riesling for a pleasant meal ending.

Serves 12

2 ¼ cups flour
1 cup sugar
1 ¼ teaspoon baking soda
½ cup butter
2 eggs
1 cup sour cream

1 teaspoon vanilla extract
¾ cup apricot preserves
⅔ cup walnuts or pecans, coarsely chopped
3 tablespoons cocoa
1 tablespoon milk

Sift together the flour, sugar and 1 teaspoon of the baking soda into a large bowl. Cut in the butter with a pastry blender or two knives until the particles are the size of peas. Beat in the eggs, sour cream, and vanilla extract with an electric mixer at low speed.

Reserve 1 cup of the batter and pour the rest of the batter into a well-greased and lightly floured 13x9x2-inch baking pan. Spread the batter with the apricot preserves and sprinkle with the nuts.

Add the cocoa, milk, and remaining ¼ teaspoon of baking soda to the reserved batter. Mix well and drop by teaspoonfuls over the preserves. Bake the cake in a preheated 350 F. degree oven for 30 to 35 minutes or until a cake tester inserted in the center comes out clean of dough. Serve with whipped cream.

Poppy Seed Cake with Chocolate Glaze

The orange flavor of this cake and its glaze is complemented by a sweet-style Riesling.

Serves 8 to 10

1 stick butter or margarine, softened
¾ cup sugar
2 large eggs
¾ cup sour cream
Grated rind of 1 orange
¼ cup fresh orange juice

⅓ cup poppy seeds
1 ½ teaspoons vanilla extract
1 ⅓ cups flour
¾ teaspoon baking powder
¾ teaspoon baking soda

Grease the bottom of an 8-inch springform pan and dust it with flour, shaking off the excess flour.

In a bowl with an electric mixer cream together the butter and sugar until light and fluffy. Beat in the eggs one at a time. Add the sour cream, orange rind, orange juice, poppy seeds and vanilla extract, beating well to blend ingredients. Combine the flour, baking powder and soda and add to the egg mixture, again beating well to combine. Pour the batter into the prepared pan and bake in a preheated 350° F. oven for 50 minutes or until a cake tester inserted in the center of the cake comes out clean. Let the cake cool, remove the pan ring and spread the chocolate glaze on top.

Chocolate Glaze

3 ounces semi-sweet chocolate
2 tablespoons butter

1 tablespoon light corn syrup
2 tablespoons Grand Marnier

Place the chocolate, butter, corn syrup and Grand Marnier in a small saucepan over very low heat. When the chocolate is melted, stir the mixture well to combine all ingredients. Spread the glaze on top of the cake.

Sauvignon Blanc

Sauvignon Blanc is considered one of the half-dozen classic wines of France. This white wine is closely associated with the Bordeaux region of southwestern France and the Sancerre/Pouilly Fumé region of the upper Loire Valley. While the vintners of the upper Loire require it to stand alone, it is most treasured in the Bordeaux region when blended with a small amount of Sémillon. California has had considerable success with Sauvignon Blanc, especially when Robert Mondavi decided to market it under the name Fumé Blanc, after taming its "grassiness" with oak aging to give it a "smoky" sensation.

Sauvignon Blanc is best consumed as a young wine, especially when vinified dry. The semi-dry versions produced around Sauterne in the Bordeaux region, however, age well over many years. The Sauvignon Blanc grape tends to be high in both acid and sugar, requiring that it be harvested at just the right balance of the two. Picked too early to capture the fruitiness causes excessive tartness, while picked later to reduce the acidity, the wine yields a flabby impression. Because of its somewhat grassy or green pepper character, Sauvignon Blanc goes particularly well with fish and shell fish.

Five Virginia wineries offer Sauvignon Blanc wine. Two of these, Barboursville Vineyards and Jefferson Vineyards, are located near Charlottesville, two, Naked Mountain Vineyards and Linden Vineyards, are near each other in northern Virginia, while Shenandoah Vineyards is in the Shenamdoah Valley near Edinburg. All of these vintners give their Sauvignon Blanc a dry finish.

Smoked Salmon Mousse

This Salmon Mousse, made in a jiffy in a food processor, makes a wonderful hors d'oeuvre. Serve it with a glass of Sauvignon Blanc, whose herbaceous flavor complements the smoky taste of the salmon.

Makes 1 cup

4 ounces smoked salmon
½ cup whipping cream
Dash of white pepper
1 teaspoon lemon juice

¼ cup melted butter
2 tablespoons fresh dill, washed,
        patted dry, and then chopped

Combine the salmon, whipping cream, and pepper in the bowl of a food processor and process until smooth. Remove salmon mixture to a bowl and fold in the lemon juice, melted butter, and dill. Place in refrigerator for at least 1 hour before serving. Serve with crackers.

Broccoli Soup

This is a good way to use broccoli stems. Three-quarters of the broccoli called for in the recipe can be peeled diced stems, cut into 1-inch pieces. The addition of rice smooths out the soup, eliminating the need for cream. Sauvignon Blanc pairs well with this soup.

Serves 6 as a first course

1 ½ tablespoon butter
1 small onion, chopped
2 stalks, celery, sliced
3 ounces crimini (brown) mushrooms, sliced
4 cups diced broccoli

2 tablespoons fresh basil, julienned
⅓ cup long grain rice
2 cups chicken broth
3 cups water

Melt the butter in a 3-quart saucepan over medium heat. Add the onion, celery, and mushrooms and sauté just until the vegetables are limp, but not browned. Add the broccoli, basil, rice, chicken broth and water. Bring to a boil and cook, covered, over medium heat until the broccoli is very tender, about 25 minutes.

Puree the soup lightly so that some tiny pieces of vegetables remain. A hand-held blender used directly in the saucepan is ideal for this, or use a food processor.

Salmon Mousse

The herbaceous flavor of a Sauvignon Blanc complements the fresh dill and the smokey taste of the salmon in this colorful mousse, which may be served as a first course or a light luncheon dish.

Serves 8

2 (6 and 1/8 ounce) cans pink salmon, well drained
1 (8 ounce) container soft cream cheese with smoked salmon
2 teaspoons lemon juice
1 English cucumber
1 envelope plus ½ teaspoon unflavored gelatin

¼ cup cold water
1 cup sour cream
½ cup chopped fresh dill
Red leaf lettuce
16 asparagus spears, blanched

With an electric mixer at medium speed beat together the salmon, cream cheese, and lemon juice in a bowl until well mixed.

Peel and seed about ¾ of the cucumber. Then puree it in a food processor only long enough so that small pieces remain. Drain the cucumber well. There should be 1 cup of cucumber; if not enough add more minced cucumber.

Soften the gelatin in cold water and stir over low heat until dissolved. Place the sour cream in another bowl and add the gelatin to it. Stir half of the sour cream mixture into the salmon. Add the cucumber and chopped dill to the remaining sour cream.

Spread half of the salmon mixture onto the bottom of a lightly oiled 4x8-inch loaf pan. Then spread the sour cream mixture over the salmon and spoon the remaining salmon over the sour cream. Chill at least four hours or overnight. Cut into 8 slices and serve each on a bed of lettuce garnished with 2 asparagus spears.

Crab Cakes

Blue fin crabs are found predominantly in the Chesapeake Bay region of Virginia and Maryland. They are used in crab cakes, crab soups, Crab Imperial, and crab salads. The addition of baking powder to this crab mixture results in a light and fluffy crab cake, which is complemented by Sauvignon Blanc.

Serves 8

1 pound crab meat
1 egg, beaten
⅔ cup finely crushed saltine cracker crumbs
1 ½ teaspoons Old Bay Seasoning
3 dashes Tabasco sauce
½ teaspoon dry mustard

1 teaspoon Worcestershire sauce
1 teaspoon baking powder
1 tablespoon lemon juice
3 tablespoons chopped parsley
3 to 4 tablespoons mayonnaise
Butter or margarine for frying

Pick over the crab meat, removing any loose shells. Place in a bowl and add all of the ingredients except the mayonnaise. Gently fold to mix, being careful not to break up the crabmeat. Fold in enough mayonnaise to hold the mixture together. Shape the crabmeat mixture into 8 three-inch patties.

Melt enough butter in a large skillet over medium heat to cover the bottom of the skillet. Add the crab cakes and fry until brown on one side, about 3 to 4 minutes, then turn and brown the other side, also about 3 to 4 minutes. Serve at once.

Shrimp Curry

Once the shrimp are shelled and deveined, this entree can be prepared in a very short time. Microwave cooking keeps the shrimp moist and the vegetables crunchy. The grassiness of a Sauvignon Blanc pairs well with the vegetables and spices used in this dish.

Serves 4

3 tablespoons butter or margarine
1 small onion, chopped
1 stalk celery, sliced
½ cup chopped green pepper
⅓ cup chopped red pepper
5 large mushrooms, sliced

2 tablespoons chopped fresh ginger
3 tablespoons flour
1 ½ teaspoons curry powder
½ cup chicken broth
½ cup milk
1 ¼ pounds medium shrimp

Shell and devein the shrimp.

In a 2 quart casserole suitable for the microwave, combine the butter, onion, celery, green and red peppers, mushrooms and ginger. Microwave on high for 4 to 5 minutes, or until the vegetables are partially cooked, stirring halfway through the cooking time,

Add the flour and curry powder and stir to mix well. Then add the chicken broth and milk, again stirring well. Add the shrimp and combine with the sauce. Cover the casserole with a glass lid or plastic wrap and microwave on high for 5 minutes, stirring halfway through the cooking time. Do not overcook the shrimp. Serve with hot rice.

Pasta with Shrimp and Tomato

Sauvignon Blanc complements this light cream-based pasta dish which is topped with lightly seasoned sautéed shrimps.

Serves 4

5 tablespoons butter or margarine
1 cup sliced crimini (brown) mushrooms
¾ cup julienned shiitake mushrooms
½ cup chopped red pepper
¾ cup chopped celery
1 large ripe tomato, peeled and diced
¾ cup dry white wine

1 cup whipping cream
2 tablespoons slivered fresh basil
10 ounces spaghettini
Salt and pepper, to taste
1 pound of large shrimp, peeled and deveined
½ teaspoon of dry Italian seasoning
Freshly grated Parmesan cheese, optional

Melt 3 tablespoons of the butter in a large skillet over medium heat and add the mushrooms, red pepper, and celery. Sauté for about 5 minutes or until the mushrooms begin to get limp. Add the tomato and continue sautéing for a few minutes. Add the wine and cook until some of the wine starts to evaporate. Then add the cream and continue cooking on low heat until the sauce starts to thicken. Add the basil and keep warm on low heat.

In the meantime, boil the spaghettini in salted water until al dente. Just before the pasta is done, melt the remaining 2 tablespoons of butter in another skillet over medium heat and add the shrimp. Sprinkle with the dry Italian seasoning and sauté for about 2 minutes on each side or until the shrimp are just done.

Drain the pasta and place into a warm bowl. Add the sauce and toss to combine. Divide the pasta among four warm plates. Top each serving with an equal amount of shrimp. Serve with grated Parmesan cheese, if desired.

Orange Roughy with Snow Peas

Orange roughy is a firm-fleshed fish from Australia and New Zealand. Usually shipped in the form of frozen fillets, it is readily available in the United States. Monk fish or any other dense, firm-fleshed fish can be substituted in this recipe. The lemon-flavored rice gives this dish another pleasing flavor that pairs well with Sauvignon Blanc.

Serves 6

2 pounds orange roughy fillets,
    cut into 1-inch-wide strips
Salt and pepper, to taste
¼ cup flour
8 tablespoons (1 stick) butter
2 leeks, white part only, cut into 2-inch
    long fine julienne (about 2 cups)

1 cup fish stock or clam juice
1 cup dry white wine
1 ½ cups whipping cream
2 cups snow peas, cleaned and cut in half
    on the bias

Season the fish strips lightly with salt and pepper and dust lightly on both sides with flour.

Heat a large skillet over medium-high heat and add 2 tablespoons of butter. Shake the fish strips to remove excess flour before adding them to the pan. Do not crowd them; half of the strips may have to be cooked at a time. Sauté the strips for about 1 minute on each side. Remove from pan and set aside.

Clean the pan, heat, and add the remaining butter. Add the leeks and sauté them over medium-high heat for 3 to 4 minutes, until limp. Do not brown them. Add the fish stock and wine, bring to a boil and cook until the liquid is reduced by half, about 10 minutes over medium high heat. Add the cream and continue cooking about 10 minutes to reduce the sauce until it coats a spoon thickly. Season with salt and pepper to taste. Add the cooked fish with any juices that have formed and the snow peas. Cook just until the fish is heated through and the snow peas are softened, about 2 minutes.

Remove from heat and serve with basmati (a fine long-grained Indian rice) or regular long-grain rice that has been cooked in chicken broth to which a little grated lemon zest has been added.

Sémillon

One of the traditional white wine grapes of the Bordeaux region of France, Sémillon is grown throughout the world. Its best characteristics, however, are brought out in cooler climes. When properly grown in the right climate zone, Sémillon makes an excellent delicate, fruity wine, best vinified off-dry or sweet. In the Bordeaux region, however, it is typically used as a blending agent with Sauvignon Blanc to tame the aggressive tartness of the latter. Sémillon (pronounced sem-ee-yon) is one of the few grapes that is susceptible to the "noble rot" (Botrytis Cinera) which yields such luscious sweet wines as French Sauterne.

Piedmont Vineyards and Afton Mountain Vineyards are the only current producer of Sémillon in Virginia. Piedmont Vineyards was the first commercial wine produced in Virginia from a Vinifera variety. When Mrs. Elizabeth Furness, founder of Piedmont Vineyards, decided to plant grapes in 1973, she selected her favorite wine variety. Alan LeBlanc-Kinne, Piedmont's wine maker, adds a small amount of Sauvignon Blanc to the wine to give it complexity since Sémillon grapes tend to be low in aroma and acidity.

Tom and Shinko Corpora at Afton Mountain Vineyards have introduced two wines based on Sémillon. One is a blend of Sémillon (67 percent) and Sauvignon Blanc (33 percent). This blend is finished off-dry. The other is a sweet dessert wine made from 100 percent Sémillon.

1993

Semillon/Sauvignon Blanc

Semillon 67% - Sauvignon Blanc 33%

VIRGINIA

Afton Mountain
VINEYARDS

ALCOHOL 12% BY VOLUME

Chicken Salad

Serve this salad for lunch or a light supper. It is a good way to use leftover chicken. The slight curry taste is balanced by the grapes and dates for a pleasant taste sensation.

Serves 4

1 ½ cups cubed cooked chicken
⅓ cup diced red pepper
½ cup diced celery
¾ cup red seedless grapes, cut in half
4 dates, cut in small cubes

½ cup chopped walnuts
¾ teaspoon curry powder
½ cup mayonnaise, or enough to
    bind the salad
Lettuce leaves

In a bowl combine the chicken, red pepper, celery, grapes, dates, and walnuts. In another bowl combine the curry powder and mayonnaise and then stir the mixture into the chicken. Add more mayonnaise, if needed and more curry powder, if desired.

To serve, place lettuce leaves on four places and top with one-fourth of the chicken salad.

Avocado Soup

This soup is good either hot or cold and freezes well, too. The Hass (California) avocados are richer in flavor than their Florida cousins.

Serves 6 as a first course

2 large Hass avocados, peeled and
    pits removed
2 ¼ cups chicken broth
1 teaspoon grated orange zest

½ cup cream
1 cup fresh orange juice
½ cup chopped tender celery

Put the avocados, 1 cup of the chicken broth, and the orange zest into the bowl of a food processor and process until a perfectly smooth paste is formed. Pour the mixture into a large bowl. Then place the other cup of chicken broth, cream, orange juice, and celery into the food processor bowl and process until the celery is very fine. Add this mixture to the avocado mass and whisk the two together until smooth. Serve either heated or cold.

Pasta with Prawn Sauce

The secret of this dish lies in the sautéing and cooking of the prawn shells that impart a wonderful flavor to the sauce. The flavor is enhanced by tomatoes, onion, garlic, wine, and cream.

Serves 6 as a first course or 4 as a main course

1 tablespoon olive oil
30 medium prawns, shelled and deveined, shells reserved
1 carrot, finely chopped
1 celery stalk, finely chopped
1 small onion, chopped
2 shallots, chopped
2 garlic cloves, minced
1 cup dry white wine
1 tomato, chopped
2 tablespoons tomato paste
1/4 cup brandy
1 tablespoon fresh tarragon, lightly chopped
1 cup whipping cream
Salt and white pepper, to taste
8 tablespoons (1 stick) butter, plus 2 tablespoons butter
12 ounces capelli d'angelo (angel hair pasta)

Heat the olive oil in a saucepan over medium-high heat until almost smoking. Reduce heat to medium and add the prawn shells, stirring quickly for a few minutes. They should turn dark red and brown in spots. Cook the shells for a few minutes. Then add the carrot, celery, onion, and shallots. Cook and stir a few more minutes. Add the wine to deglaze the pan and reduce the liquid by half. Then add the tomato, tomato paste, brandy and tarragon and simmer the mixture for 20 to 25 minutes.

Remove from the heat and place the sauce in a food processor. Process until smooth and the shells are in very fine pieces. Press the mixture through a fine sieve, extracting all of the juices possible. Return the sauce mixture to a saucepan, add the cream, salt and pepper, and simmer for 10 minutes. Add 8 tablespoons of the butter, a little at a time, whisking until thoroughly combined. (It is not necessary to use all of the butter called for, although the full measure makes the sauce rich and tasty)

To assemble the dish, heat the remaining 2 tablespoons of butter in a sauté pan over high heat. Add the prawns to the pan and sauté until deep pink, but not rubbery, about 4 minutes. Remove the prawns from the pan and keep them warm.

Cook the pasta al dente, about 3 to 4 minutes, in boiling salted water with a little olive oil in it to keep the strands from sticking together. Drain the pasta and add it to the sauce.

Place the pasta on warm plates, pour a little extra sauce over each serving, and arrange 5 prawns on top of the pasta.

Linzer Torte

The hazelnuts in the dough and the raspberry jam in the filling made this Viennese torte famous. It pairs well with a semi-sweet Sémillon.

Serves 8 to 10

4 cups flour
1 pound hazelnuts, lightly toasted,
   skins removed, and then ground
3 ¼ cups confectioners sugar
1 pound butter

1 whole egg
2 egg yolks
1 teaspoon powdered cinnamon
Zest of 1 lemon, grated
1 ½ cups raspberry or black currant jam

Butter a 10-inch springform pan that is 2 inches high.

In a bowl combine the flour, ground hazelnuts, and sugar. Cut in the butter with a pastry blender until it resembles small peas. Add the egg, 1 egg yolk, cinnamon, and lemon zest. Combine the mixture until it forms a dough. Wrap dough in plastic wrap and store in refrigerator for 20 minutes.

Using your fingers press three-quarters of the dough into the bottom and up the sides of the pan. Spread the jam over the dough.

Roll out the remaining dough 1/4-inch thick and cut it into strips. Crisscross the strips over the filling for a lattice effect. Beat the remaining egg yolk and carefully brush it over the strips. Bake in a preheated 350° F. oven for 45 minutes or until the crust is nicely browned. Allow to cool, unmold and serve.

Seyval Blanc

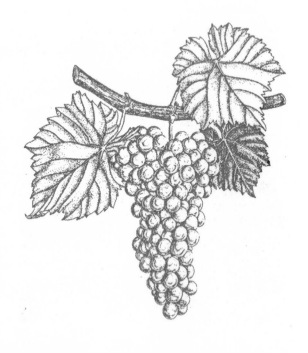

Developed in 1921 by Alfred Seibel, the premier French hybridizer, Seyval has become the most popular of the French hybrids grown in the eastern United States. Vintners like Seyval because the vines are winter hardy, highly productive, and resistant to disease. One of the disadvantages of Seyval is that it buds early and, therefore, is subject to damage from late spring frosts.

Seyval yields a crisp fruity wine, even in cool climates. When it was first introduced in America, enthusiasts called it "the Chardonnay of the East," and vintners produced Seyval in the style of French Chablis—dry and moderately oaky. Today vintners produce it in a wide range of styles, from dry to sweet and austere to moderately oaked. It is also produced as a late harvest dessert wine.

There are eleven producers of Seyval in Virginia, ranging from Chateau Morrisette, high on the crest of the Blue Ridge Mountains south of Roanoke, to Ingleside Plantation Vineyards on the tidelands of Northern Neck. Many Virginia vintners finish their Seyval wines as they do Riesling, with an off-dry finish, while others treat it like Chardonnay with a dry finish.

Vintners also vary in their use of oak in the finishing of Seyval. Bill Heidig, co-owner of Lake Anna Winery, favors handling his Seyval in stainless steel, bottling both a dry and off-dry Seyval, with the latter containing modest amounts of Chardonnay and Riesling. Deer Meadow, Swedenburg Winery, and Chateau Morrisette, among others, add a touch of complexity to their Seyval by aging in oak for several months, while Archie Smith III at Meredyth Vineyards both ferments and ages his Seyval in oak barrels. Shep Rouse at Oakencroft also ages Seyval in oak. He bottles it under the Countryside White label.

Peanut Soup

In 1794 Thomas Jefferson's garden contained 65 peanut hills. Generally, however, the nuts were considered a novelty until after the Civil War. They were used principally by the Negro slave cooks when cooking for themselves, although occasionally in dishes for their masters. Peanut Soup, a Virginia specialty, was one of the few peanut-based dishes enjoyed by the colonists. Serve with an oak-aged Seyval.

Serves 4 to 6

4 tablespoons (½ stick) butter or margarine
⅓ cup very finely minced onion
⅓ cup very finely minced celery
1 ½ tablespoons flour

1 cup smooth peanut butter
½ cup half and half
Salt and pepper, to taste
¼ cup chopped peanuts, for garnish

Melt the butter in a large saucepan over medium-low heat. Add the onions and celery and sauté until soft, but not brown. Stir in the flour and blend until smooth. Lower heat to simmer and stir in the peanut butter. Slowly add the chicken broth, bring to a slow boil, and simmer the soup for 20 minutes. Add the half and half and heat the soup just to the boiling point. Add salt and pepper, to taste. Ladle the soup into bowls and garnish each serving with some chopped peanuts.

Greek Salad

This colorful salad may be served as a first course or as a light luncheon dish. It is best served at room temperature so that the flavors have had a chance to meld.

Serves 6

3 tomatoes, cut into chunks
1 green pepper, cut into slices
1 red pepper, cut into slices
1 medium onion, cut into slices
½ cup Kalamata olives
½ pound feta cheese, cut into 1/4-inch dice

8 large basil leaves, cut into shreds,
    or 1 tablespoon dried basil
Salt and pepper, to taste
¼ cup olive oil
1 tablespoons red wine vinegar
1 tablespoon red wine

In a large bowl combine the vegetables. olives, cheese, and seasonings. Then combine the olive oil, vinegar, and wine, and pour over the salad. Toss gently to mix. Let the salad sit at room temperature for one hour to meld the flavors.

Greens Soup

Greens soup is English in origin and was probably brought to Virginia by the Scotch and English who settled here. This modern version combines collard greens with kale for a mild flavor. Serve the soup with crusty French bread and a glass of Seyval.

Serves 6

1 cup dry small white (Navy) beans	1 pound collard greens
3 slices bacon, cut into 1-inch pieces	1 pound kale
1 pound smoked sausage, such as	⅓ cup chopped red pepper
Kielbasa, cut into 1-inch slices	1 medium potato, peeled and cut in
1 medium onion, chopped	small cubes
2 cups chicken broth	Salt and pepper, to taste
6 cups water	

Place the beans in a saucepan and add 3 cups water. Bring to a boil and boil for two minutes. Remove the beans from the heat and cover the saucepan. Let the beans stand for 1 hour.

Cook the bacon in a large skillet over medium heat. When some of the fat has been rendered, add the sausage and onion. Sauté for 5 minutes until the onions are transparent and the sausage has started to brown.

With a slotted spoon remove the sausage, bacon, and onion to a large soup pot. Drain the beans and add them with the chicken broth and water to the soup pot. Bring to a slow boil and continue cooking over low heat for 1 hour.

In the meantime remove the center stem from the collard greens and kale. Wash the greens and shred them into bite-sized pieces. Add the greens to the soup and continue cooking over low for 45 minutes. Then add the red pepper and potatoes and cook another 20 minutes on medium heat, or until the potatoes are soft. Season to taste with salt and pepper.

Zucchini Stuffed Chicken with Potatoes

Zucchini is a member of the summer squash family, being called green squash in some areas. It, like all other squash, is American in origin, but was not the most popular of the variety in the New World. The green squash, brought back to Europe by an early explorer, first made a name for itself in Italy. Thus the rest of the world has come to regard zucchini as Italian squash. It is used in this recipe as a stuffing for baked chicken.

Serves 4

1 ½ cup chopped spinach
1 cup shredded zucchini
3 large mushrooms, shredded
1 small onion, chopped
⅓ cup freshly grated Parmesan cheese
½ cup soft white bread crumbs
¼ teaspoon dried thyme
¼ teaspoon salt
¼ teaspoon pepper

1 chicken (about 3 ½ to 4 pounds)
Salt and pepper, to taste
Garlic powder
Onion powder
Paprika
4 medium new red potatoes, cut into
    ¾ inch slices
2 tablespoons butter

Combine the spinach, zucchini, mushrooms, onion, cheese, bread crumbs, thyme, salt, and pepper.

Lightly stuff the cavity of the chicken with the vegetable mixture. Place the chicken in a large flat casserole and sprinkle it with salt, pepper, garlic powder, onion powder, and paprika. Place the potatoes around the chicken and sprinkle them with a little onion powder and paprika. Dot the potatoes and chicken with the 2 tablespoons of butter. Bake in a preheated 400° F. oven for 1 ¼ hours.

Thai Salad

Leftovers become the basis of an Oriental salad of Thai origin. Other vegetables may be added to the stir-fry, if desired. Serve this salad for a luncheon or light summer dinner with a glass of Seyval.

Serves 4

Dressing

⅔ cup dry white wine

2 tablespoons smooth peanut butter

3 tablespoons sesame oil

3 tablespoon soy sauce

¼ teaspoon hot oil

½ teaspoon lime juice

Combine the dressing ingredients in a small bowl and whisk until very smooth.

Salad

1½ cups julienned strips of leftover roast
     beef, pork loin, or chicken

Half of an 8-ounce package of Chinese noodles

1 tablespoon vegetable oil

1 red pepper, julienned

1 large carrot, julienned

¾ cup sliced cremini (brown) mushrooms

¼ cup sliced shiitake mushrooms

1 (8 ounces) can sliced water chestnuts

3 green onions, thinly sliced

1 tablespoon finely minced ginger

2 cups thinly sliced Napa cabbage

Chopped peanuts, for garnish

Boil the noodles in lightly salted boiling water for 3 minutes. Drain them and toss with a little of the dressing so that the noodles do not stick together.

Heat the vegetable oil in a skillet; add the pepper, carrot, water chestnuts, onions, and ginger, and stir-fry for 4 to 5 minutes or until the vegetables are still crisp-tender. Add the meat and heat through. Mound the cabbage on a large platter. Top with the noodles and then the stir-fry. Pour the dressing over and garnish with chopped peanuts.

Steuben

The Steuben American hybrid was developed at New York state's Geneva Research Station in 1947. The attractive blue-black grape produces a pleasant rosé and a muscat-like wine with a slight Labrusca undertone. Steuben pairs well with spicy foods, particularly with Cajun and Creole dishes.

Deer Meadow Vineyard, southwest of Winchester, is the only grower and producer of Steuben wine. Charles Sarle, co-owner and wine maker at Deer Meadow makes two Steuben-based wines, a semi-dry wine with lovely color, labeled Golden Blush, and a dessert wine containing a blend of Steuben and Seyval with a sugar content of 3 percent. Even with the Seyval and high sugar, the floral bouquet of the Steuben still stands out.

Chinese Vegetable Dip

This simple-to-prepare dip is seasoned with spices and chutney. It will keep in the refrigerator for 3 to 4 days.

Makes 3 cups

2 cups sour cream
¾ teaspoon Chinese Five Spice seasoning
½ cup unsalted, dry-roasted, chopped
　　peanuts

3 teaspoons chopped onion
½ cup chutney

Combine the above ingredients and chill thoroughly. Serve with bite-size pieces of broccoli, cauliflower, celery sticks, or zucchini sticks.

Creole Jambalaya

This version of Jambalaya incorporates many of the ingredients of Creole cookery. The type of ingredients in a jambalaya can vary, but must always include rice.

The use of diced chicken breasts instead of chicken pieces in this recipe reduces the cooking time. More readily available mild Italian sausage is used in this recipe, although Andouille sausage would give this jambalaya a sweeter flavor. The muscat-like flavor of the Steuben wine adds to the enjoyment of this dish.

Serves 4

1 tablespoon butter
6 ounces sweet Italian sausages,
    cut into 1-inch pieces
12 ounces boned and skinned chicken breasts,
    cut into 1-inch pieces
¼ cup chopped red pepper
¼ cup chopped green pepper
1 jalapeño pepper, seeded and chopped
1 medium onion, chopped
1 clove garlic, chopped
2 large tomatoes, peeled, seeded and chopped
8 large okra, cut into 1-inch pieces

1 cup medium-grain rice
1 ½ cups chicken broth
1 ½ cups water
¼ teaspoon dried thyme
¼ bay leaf
⅛ teaspoon ground cloves
A pinch of red pepper flakes
1 teaspoon paprika
6 ounces boiled ham, cut into 1-inch pieces
6 ounces medium shrimp, shelled and
    deveined
⅓ cup chopped parsley

Melt the butter in a large, deep skillet over medium heat. Add the sausage and lightly brown the pieces on both sides. Remove the sausage and add the chicken pieces and lightly brown them; then remove. Add the peppers, onions, and garlic, and sauté until the vegetables are no longer crisp, 3 to 5 minutes. Add the tomato, okra, rice, chicken broth, water, and seasonings. Bring to a boil, reduce heat, cover, and cook over low heat for 18 to 20 minutes, or until the rice is barely done. Return the chicken and sausage to the pan along with the ham, shrimp, and parsley. Continue cooking for 5 to 7 minutes, or until the chicken and shrimp are done and the ingredients are heated through.

Gingerbread with Apricot Glaze

Gingerbread has been served in America since colonial times. It was Martha Washington's favorite dessert. This moist gingerbread is topped with an apricot-sherry glaze. Serve with a glass of dessert wine such as Steuben.

Serves 10 to 12

½ cup sugar
¼ teaspoon salt
½ teaspoon ground ginger
¼ teaspoon cinnamon
¼ teaspoon ground cloves
¼ teaspoon nutmeg
½ cup vegetable oil

½ cup dark molasses
1 teaspoon baking soda
¼ cup boiling water
¼ cup cream sherry
1 ¼ cups flour
1 egg, beaten

Combine the sugar, salt and spices in a bowl. Stir in the oil and molasses, blending well. Mix together the soda, and the boiling water and stir into the sugar mixture. Then add the cream sherry and pour in the flour in a gradual stream, stirring constantly to prevent lumps. Add the beaten egg and mix well. Pour the batter into a well-greased 8-by 8-inch pan and bake in a preheated 350° F. oven for 30 to 35 minutes. Spoon the glaze over the warm cake and serve at room temperature.

Glaze

1 cup apricot jam
⅓ cup water
1 teaspoon sugar

1 teaspoon grated orange zest
2 tablespoons cream sherry
½ chopped walnuts

Combine the apricot jam, water, sugar, and orange zest in a small saucepan. Bring to a boil and simmer for 5 minutes, stirring constantly. Remove from the heat and stir in the sherry and walnuts.

Trebbiano

One of the world's most prolific grape producers, Trebbiano (called Ugni Blanc in France) is a white grape native to central Italy. Popular as a varietal wine in Italy it is also used in both France and Italy as the base wine of cognac and other brandies. Wine made from the Trebbiano grape is pale lemon in color, has little aroma but high acidity, and has modest body and fruitiness.

Steve Haskell at Villa Appalaccia near the Blue Ridge Parkway in southern Virginia is the only grower of the Trebbiano grape in Virginia. He plans to produce Trebbiano wine within the next year.

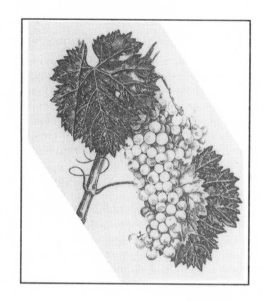

Cheese Ball

Cheese balls are always a welcome addition to a cocktail hour and they can be made in advance. A glass of delicate Trebbiano goes well with this cream cheese hors d'oeuvre.

Makes 1 (8 ounce) ball

1 (8 ounce package) cream cheese,
    chilled and cut into 6 pieces
⅓ cup stuffed green olives, well drained

½ teaspoon Italian seasonings
¼ teaspoon onion powder
¾ cup chopped parsley

Place the cream cheese, olives, Italian seasonings, and onion powder in the bowl of a food processor. Pulse to mix all ingredients. It may be necessary to stop and stir the mixture once or twice. Turn the mixture onto a piece of wax paper; mound into a ball and gather the wax paper around it. Place the cheese ball in the freezer until firm but not frozen, about 40 minutes. Remove the wax paper and roll the cheese ball in chopped parsley. Wrap in wax paper or plastic wrap and refrigerate until ready to serve. Serve with crackers.

Porcini Risotto with Red and Yellow Peppers

This version of Risotto is rich and full of flavor and can easily be served as a separate course. If dried porcini mushrooms are not available, any other dried mushrooms may be substituted. The flavor, however, will be slightly different. This recipe may also be prepared with 4 ounces each of shiitake and crimini (brown) mushrooms. If doing so, proceed with the recipe by sautéing the mushrooms with the pepper strips and substitute chicken broth for the mushroom liquid. Italian Arborio rice, a short, thick grained rice, is available in gourmet shops. Serve this risotto as a first course or as an accompaniment to grilled meats.

Serves 8

1 ½ ounces dried porcini mushrooms
8 tablespoon (1 stick) unsalted butter
1 cup julienned red bell pepper
1 cup julienned yellow pepper
1 cup chopped sweet red onion
2 large cloves garlic, minced
2 cups Italian Arborio rice

3 to 4 cups hot chicken broth
1 cup dry white wine
½ teaspoon freshly ground black pepper
1 cup whipping cream
1 cup freshly grated Parmesan cheese
Salt to taste, if needed

Place the porcini mushrooms in a small bowl and cover with boiling water. Let stand for 30 minutes. Remove the porcini and coarsely chop them. Strain the liquid through a fine cloth and reserve it for use in gravies or soup stock.

Melt 4 tablespoons of the butter in a large heavy saucepan over medium heat. Add the red and yellow peppers and the mushrooms; sauté for 2 minutes. Remove with a slotted spoon and set aside. Melt the remaining butter in the same saucepan. Add the onion and garlic and sauté for about 3 minutes until the onion is translucent. Mix in the rice, stirring for about 2 minutes until the rice is well coated with the butter.

Stir in 2 cups of the chicken broth, wine, and freshly ground pepper. Cook uncovered over low heat until the liquid is almost absorbed. Stir occasionally. Continue adding chicken broth, half a cup at a time, until the rice is almost al dente. Stir in the cream and continue cooking and stirring until the mixture is thick and creamy. The rice will take a total of about 30 to 35 minutes to become tender. Stir in the vegetables and cheese and adjust seasonings, if necessary. The finished risotto will have a creamy consistency.

Vidal Blanc

A hybrid developed in France to provide a grape that produces high sugar content in cooler climates, Vidal is a good producer and is disease-resistant. Its parents include Trebbiano (Ugni Blanc in France) and a Siebel French hybrid named Rayon d'Or (grown by Guilford Ridge Vineyard in Virginia). Vidal Blanc produces good acid levels that provide a balance with the fruitiness and sugar. Wine from this grape has a gentle-fruity character. Vidal Blanc is a very friendly grape from the vintners standpoint as it can be made in both a sweet or dry style and with or without oak aging.

Vidal has become very popular with Virginia vintners because of its hardiness in the vineyard and flexibility in the winery. Fourteen Virginia wineries currently offer a varietal Vidal wine while several others use it in their blended wines. Most of the wineries ferment their Vidal in stainless steel jacketed tanks and give the wine an off-dry finish with little or no aging. Shephard "Shep" Rouse at Rockbridge Vineyard ferments and ages his Vidal Blanc in oak barrels. Shep's Vidal-based wine is actually a blend of five-sixth Vidal and one-sixth Riesling, and is bottled under a St. Mary's Blanc label. Oakencroft Vineyards, where Shep is also winemaker, makes a sweet Vidal, called Sweet Virginia, with 5 percent residual sugar. Oakencroft also uses Vidal Blanc in its blush wine, although it contains small amounts of Chambourcin for color, and Seyval. Grey Ghost, a new winery in Amissville, finishes its Vidal dry.

Jim Law at Linden Vineyards makes an off-dry combination of Vidal and Riesling which is cold fermented in stainless steel tanks and bottled with no aging. The Vidal gives the wine a Gewürztraminer-like spiciness, while the Riesling adds a fruity component. When conditions permit, Jim also makes a late harvest Vidal dessert wine. The grapes are kept on the vine until after the first frost and usually picked in November, which intensifies the sugar and spiciness of the extracted juice. The juice is kept cold in a jacketed tank to extend fermentation through the winter months.

Ham and Potato Chowder

Chowders first became a part of American cooking in New England where they were made with fish. Later in the Midwest chowders were created with readily available smoked pork, potatoes, and other vegetables.

This chowder is a good way to use the last of a ham and the ham bone. Small pieces of fresh green beans are added at the end of the cooking time. For a variation add fresh corn kernels during the last 7 minutes of cooking.

Serves 6

5 large carrots, diced
4 stalks celery, diced
1 medium onion, diced
5 large potatoes, diced
6 cups water
¼ teaspoon pepper

½ teaspoon dried thyme
1 ham bone
¾ cup 1-inch pieces of green beans
2 cups diced ham
⅓ cup half and half

Place the carrots, celery, onion, and potatoes in a stock pot and add the water, pepper, and thyme. Bring to a boil and cook over medium-low heat for 25 minutes, or until the vegetables are tender. Mash about half of the vegetables with a potato masher. Add the ham bone and bring the soup back to a boil. Then continue simmering for 2 ½ to 3 hours. Add the green beans and cook on medium-low heat for 15 to 20 minutes, or until the beans are done. Add the ham and the half and half to smooth and thin the soup. Heat through and serve.

Roast Loin of Pork with Prune and Apple Stuffing

The fruit stuffing of this pork roast has a pleasing contrast of sweet prunes and tart apple, flavored with ginger. Cooking the roast in a combination of apple cider and the juice from the prunes adds yet another flavor component.

Serves 8

8 ounces pitted prunes
1 cup hot water
1 large tart apple, cut into ½-inch cubes
1 whole boneless pork loin
1 teaspoon ground ginger

¾ teaspoon salt
½ teaspoon pepper
3 tablespoons butter
1 cup apple cider
2 tablespoons flour dissolved in ⅓ cup water

Quarter the prunes and soak them in the hot water for 30 minutes. Drain and reserve the liquid. Combine the prunes and apple.

Cut the pork loin open lengthwise, but do not cut through. Sprinkle the meat with the salt, pepper, and ginger. Arrange the fruit down the center of the meat. Roll the roast and tie it in several places.

Melt the butter in a heavy skillet or roasting pan. Add the pork loin and brown it on all sides. Then add the apple cider and the reserved prune liquid. Cover the pan and bake in a preheated 350° F. oven for 1 ½ to 1 ¾ hours, or until the roast is done. Remove the roast to a platter and thicken the gravy with the flour and water combination.

Mincemeat Pie

Mincemeat pie is a traditional English Christmas dessert that came to America with the first settlers. In early colonial days the making of mincemeat was also a way of preserving meat and the pie was often served as part of the main course. Today mincemeat is available already prepared. The addition of candied fruit and spices cuts the richness of the prepared mincemeat used in this recipe. A Late Harvest Vidal complements the fruit and spices in this dessert.

Serves 8

1 jar (27 ounces) mincemeat
1 tart apple, peeled and shredded
2 tablespoons diced candied mixed fruit
2 tablespoons diced candied lemon peel
2 tablespoons diced candied citron
2 tablespoons orange juice
1 tablespoon lemon juice

2 tablespoons brandy
2 tablespoons dry sherry
½ teaspoon cinnamon
½ teaspoon nutmeg
½ teaspoon coriander
Pastry (recipe follows)

In a bowl combine the mincemeat and the rest of the ingredients, except the pastry. Mix well and cover with plastic wrap. Let stand for 24 hours.

Pastry

2 cups all-purpose flour
5 tablespoons butter or margarine

4 tablespoons solid vegetable shortening
4 to 5 tablespoons ice water

Place the flour in a bowl. Cut in the butter and shortening until the flour mixture has the texture of coarse crumbs. Add the water, a tablespoon at a time, and mix with a fork until the dough can be formed into a ball. Wrap dough in plastic wrap and chill for at least 1 hour.

Roll out half the dough and fit it into a 9-inch pie plate. Add the mincemeat filling. Roll out the remaining pastry and cut it into 10 strips. Place the strips on top of the filling in a lattice pattern. Bake in a preheated 425° F. oven for 35 to 40 minutes or until the crust is brown and the filling is bubbly.

Villard Blanc

Created by a French hybridizers in 1924, Villard Blanc thrives in warm climates where it is highly productive with large grape clusters. The grapes produce a fruity table wine that can be enjoyed young. It remains popular in France as an everyday wine.

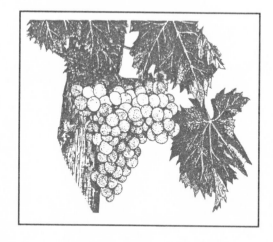

The only vintner in Virginia that currently produces a Villard Blanc-based wine is Al Weed at Mountain Cove Vineyard. His Mountain Cove Dry White is primarily Villard Blanc with a slight amount of Chardonnay added to give the wine complexity. He also bottles an off-dry blush wine called Skyline Rosé consisting of Villard Blanc with a touch of Chancellor to give the wine color.

Split Pea and Barley Soup

A hearty soup with green split-peas, barley, and brown rice for cold winter evenings. Spinach adds color and a light touch.

Serves 6

1 tablespoons butter or margarine
12 ounces kielbasa, cut in half, then sliced ½ inch thick
1 medium onion, chopped
1 leek, including light green part, chopped
1 cup dried split green peas, picked over and rinsed
1 cup barley

⅓ cup brown rice
1 medium red potato, unpeeled and cubed
1/4 teaspoon pepper
1 teaspoon dried thyme
4 cups chicken broth
4 cups water
1 ½ cups coarsely shredded spinach

Melt the butter in a stock pot. Add the kielbasa, onion, and leek and sauté until the sausage is lightly browned and the onion is limp. Add the remaining ingredients except the spinach. Cover the pot, bring to a boil, and then cook over low heat for 1 hour until the peas and barely are done. Add the spinach and continue cooking for another 4 to 5 minutes until the spinach is limp.

Baked Fillet of Flounder

When the first settlers came to Jamestown, flounder were so abundant that they could be scooped up by hand. They found them similar to the European sole. Enjoy it with a glass of French hybrid, Villard Blanc.

Serves 6

4 tablespoons butter or margarine
¼ cup chopped red onion
6 flounder fillets (about 2 pounds)
2 tablespoons tarragon mustard

3 ½ tablespoons dry white wine
½ cup freshly grated Parmesan cheese
½ cup bread crumbs

Melt 2 tablespoons of the butter and coat a flat baking dish large enough to hold the fish in a single layer. Distribute the chopped onion evenly over the bottom of the dish. Place the fish on top of the onion.

In a small dish combine the mustard with the wine. Then brush each fillet with the mustard mixture. Sprinkle with the Parmesan cheese and bread crumbs. Dot with the remaining 2 tablespoons of butter. Bake in a preheated 425° F. oven for 5 to 8 minutes, or until the fish is barely done. Place the fish under the broiler for a minute or two, until lightly browned. Serve immediately.

Chicken Breasts en Papillote

This recipe is a re-creation of an Italian dish. Although "en papillote," a French cooking term, means baking something in (parchment) paper, a double thickness of aluminum foil works just as well. It allows the chicken to steam and absorb the flavors of the aromatic juices of the herbs and vegetables.

Serves 4

2 whole boned, skinned chicken breasts, halved and pounded to about ½-inch thickness
Salt and pepper, to taste
Olive oil for brushing aluminum foil
1 tablespoon olive oil
1 shallot, minced
1 large clove garlic, minced

10 ounces shiitake mushrooms, stems removed and sliced
½ teaspoon chopped fresh rosemary or ¼ teaspoon dried
¼ teaspoon dried thyme
3 medium tomatoes, peeled, seeded, and chopped
Zest of 1 lemon

Sprinkle the chicken pieces lightly with salt and pepper.

Cut 4 large double thickness of aluminum foil, large enough to fold loosely over each piece of chicken breast. Brush the center of the aluminum with oil where the chicken will be placed and put the chicken on it.

Heat the 1 tablespoon of oil in a large skillet and sauté the shallot and garlic until the shallot is tender, but not brown. Add the mushrooms and sauté, stirring often, until the mushrooms begin to release some of their liquid. Add the rosemary, thyme, and tomatoes and cook over medium heat, stirring occasionally, for another 5 minutes. Remove from the heat and stir in the lemon zest. Season to taste with salt and pepper, if necessary.

Spoon ¼ of the sauce over each chicken breast. Fold the foil over the chicken and crimp the edges tightly together. Bake in a preheated 375° F. oven for 20 minutes. Serve in the foil.

Viognier

A seldom-found varietal, Viognier is grown primarily in the upper Rhone Valley of France, frequently intermingled with Marsanne. While producing an intriguing wine, Viognier is not cultivated extensively because the vine is a low producer and requires considerable care in cultivation. Many wine connoisseurs, however, consider wine from the Viognier grape as exceptional when the grapes are properly cultivated and converted into wine. Viognier from the Condrieu appellation in France is often sighted as the best example of this wine.

The grape produces a full-bodied golden wine with blossom, apricot, peach, and spicy undertones. While traditionally barrel fermented and then aged for a short period of time, Viognier is best enjoyed while still young. Because of its potential excellence, a number of California vintners have begun to experiment with this temperamental grape.

Dennis Horton at Horton Vineyards is the only vintner in Virginia growing and producing Viognier wine having planted 8.5 acres in 1991, plus an additional 10 acres in 1992. Horton processes the grapes into wine in the traditional French method of fermenting the wine in oak barrels and then aging it in barrels for six months.

Baked Brie with Lobster

Traditional Maine lobster is the main ingredient of a salad that is served on top of a warmed wheel of Brie. The combination makes an elegant and unique hors d'oeuvre or first course. The Viognier varietal wine matches well with the soft cheese and shell fish combination.

Serves 8 to 10 as hors d'oeuvres or 4 as a first course

1 ½ cups cooked lobster meat, cut in
    bite-size cubes
2 scallions, finely chopped
½ teaspoon celery seeds
¼ teaspoon white pepper

½ cup mayonnaise
1 small wheel of Brie, weighing
    about 14 ounces, at room temperature
Lettuce leaves, for garnish

Combine the lobster meat, scallions, celery seeds, pepper, and mayonnaise in a bowl. Refrigerate until ready to serve.

Just before serving, place the Brie on a non-stick baking sheet and top with the lobster salad. Bake in a preheated 350° F. oven for 3 minutes or until the salad is lukewarm and the cheese begins to soften.

Serve on lettuce leaves. Cut the cheese into wedges and serve as an hors d'oeuvres with crackers or as a first course with mini slices of French bread.

Quiche Lorraine

This quiche is typical of those served in the Lorraine region of France as it contains crisp bacon and Gruyère cheese. It may be served as a first course or as a luncheon entree.

Serves 4 to 6

Pastry

1 cup all-purpose flour
3 tablespoons butter or margarine
3 tablespoons solid vegetable shortening

3 to 4 tablespoons ice water
1 egg yolk
1 teaspoon Worcestershire sauce

Place the flour in a bowl. With a pastry blender cut in the butter and shortening until the solids are the size of very small peas. Fluff the mixture with a fork. Add the ice water, one tablespoon at a time, tossing the mixture with the fork until the dough sticks together and can be formed into a ball. Wrap the dough in plastic wrap and place in the refrigerator for at least one hour.

Remove dough from the refrigerator, place on a floured board, and roll 1 inch larger in diameter than the top surface of 9-inch quiche pan. Place dough in the pan; crimp the edges. Line the pan with aluminum foil, shiny side down, weight it with beans or pie weights and bake in a preheated 425 degree oven for 10 minutes. Carefully remove the pie weights and the aluminum foil. Beat together the egg yolk and Worcestershire sauce and lightly brush the mixture over the bottom of the pie crust. Bake for another 5 minutes. Cool the crust slightly while preparing the filling. Reduce the oven heat to 350 degrees.

Filling

4 eggs
1 tablespoon flour
⅔ cup half and half
⅓ cup whipping cream
1 ½ cup grated Gruyère or Swiss cheese
3 slices bacon, fried and cut into 1-inch pieces

½ cup chopped ham
½ cup broccoli florets, cut in small pieces
   and blanched for 2 minutes
¼ teaspoon pepper
Dash of cayenne pepper

In a bowl mix together the eggs, flour, half and half, and whipping cream. Stir in the cheese, bacon, ham, broccoli and peppers. Pour the filling into the prepared quiche pan. Bake in the 350° F. oven for about 45 minutes or until the filling has set and is nicely browned. Serve warm or at room temperature.

Chicken and Chestnuts

At one time edible chestnut trees were plentiful in this country, particularly in the east. Most of these trees, however, were killed in 1904 by a disease brought into the country with some Chinese chestnut trees. Efforts are now being made to grow edible chestnuts in Virginia as well as in several other states.

Serves 4

3 slices bacon, cut into 1-inch pieces
1 medium onion, chopped
1 cup sliced mushrooms
2 ½ tablespoons butter or margarine
1 frying chicken (3 to 3 ½ pounds), cut-up
Salt and pepper, to taste
1 teaspoon dried rosemary, crumbled

½ teaspoon dried thyme, crumbled
¾ cup medium (Golden) sherry
⅓ cup chicken broth
10 chestnuts, skinned and peeled (see method below)
Flour and water for gravy thickening, optional

Gently fry the bacon in a large skillet or flameproof casserole until most of the fat is rendered. Add the onions and mushrooms. Sauté until soft, about 3 to 4 minutes. Remove the vegetables and bacon bits and drain the fat from the pan.

Add 1 ½ tablespoons of the butter to the skillet and, when melted, add the chicken pieces. Brown them on both sides. Then sprinkle each piece of chicken with salt, pepper, rosemary, and thyme. Top the chicken pieces with the mushroom mixture. Combine the sherry and chicken broth and gently pour the liquid over the chicken. Cover and place in a preheated 325° F. oven for 30 minutes.

Melt the remaining tablespoon of butter in a small skillet and add the chestnut halves, tossing them lightly and taking care that they do not brown. Add the chestnuts to the chicken casserole, cover, and return it to the oven. Continue baking the chicken for another 25 to 30 minutes or until tender. Thicken the pan juices with a little flour and water, if desired.

Chestnut Preparation

Cut the chestnuts in half, vertically. Place them in a small saucepan and cover with water. Bring to a boil and boil over medium-high heat for 7 to 8 minutes. Drain and, as soon as the chestnuts are cool enough to handle, remove the outer shell and the skin.

CHAMPAGNES

Champagne

Throughout the world sparkling wine is frequently referred to as champagne, regardless of where it is produced. Correctly speaking the term "champagne" should only be applied to sparkling wine produced in the Champagne region of France by the traditional *méthode champenoise* technique.

Champagne is no longer merely a celebration wine, as it has also become a food wine. Like two close friends, food and champagne support each other in a variety of ways. It has long been a companion of hors d'oeuvres, but now provides special enjoyment with breakfast, lunch, and dinner dishes. The bubbles and the acidity inherent in champagne create a sensation on the palate that gives it sufficient zestiness to stand up to such still-wine killers as oysters and caviar. Yet its taste and aroma are delicate enough to enhance light dishes based on fish, poultry, cheese, and fruit.

The traditional process of making champagne, called *méthode champenoise*, is like making two wines in one. While various steps of the process have been mechanized, the basic technique has remained the same for almost 200 years. The first step involves fermenting the base wines completely dry in the standard manner for still wines. Today this is usually carried out in a temperature-controlled stainless steel tank. The champagne maker then prepares a blend of separately-fermented wines to achieve the desired *cuveé*. He or she adds sugar and yeast in precise amounts to the *cuveé,* which is then bottled and sealed with a temporary pressure-resistant cap. The bottles are then laid on their side while the second fermentation

103

takes place and aging occurs—generally anywhere from one-to-ten years depending on the delicacy desired in the final product.

The second fermentation creates carbon dioxide (CO_2), which builds up pressure in the bottle and produces the bubbles (In fermenting still wine, the CO_2 is allowed to dissipate into the atmosphere.) When aging is complete the bottles are slowly tipped downward so that the spent yeast, called lees, moves into the neck of the bottle. The neck is then partially frozen and the temporary cap removed to allow the pressure to disgorge the spent yeast. The champagne lost in the disgorging is immediately replaced with still wine, and the bottle is then corked, washed, labeled, and boxed for shipping.

The traditional grapes used to make the base wines for champagne in the Champagne region are Chardonnay, Pinot Noir, and Pinot Meunier. Other grape varieties are used by vintners elsewhere, such as Riesling, Gewürtztraminer, and Chenin Blanc. When using red grapes, the winemaker extracts the juice from the press immediately after pressing to keep the juice free of color and tannins. Champagne made from white grapes is usually labeled *Blanc de Blanc*, while that from red grapes as *Blanc de Noir*.

Styles of Champagne

In matching sparkling wine with food, it is important to select the proper style, which is based on the approximate amount of sugar in the champagne. Brut champagne, which is off-dry, is the most popular champagne in both Europe and America, although truly dry champagnes are becoming more popular. In making a sugarless champagne, the champagne maker must anticipate the exact amount of sugar needed during the second fermentation. He or she must also balance the acid and fruitiness of the base wines in the *cuveé*. Historically, imbalances were masked by the use of additional sugar.

The label designations used in America for the various styles of champagne conform roughly to those developed in Europe centuries ago. In terms of residual sugar content, they are as follows: Natural (0 - 0.6 percent); Brut (0.5 - 1.5 percent); Extra Dry (1.0 - 2.0 percent); Dry (1.7 - 4.0 percent); Semi-dry (3.3 - 6.0 percent); and Sweet (5.0 percent and above). The ranges of sugar content shown are only approximate as each champagne producer has its own variations of these definitions.

Today, these terms are confusing to many people because they were created over a century ago when sweet champagnes were in vogue throughout Europe. The designations came into common use when the term "dry" meant any champagne with less than 4 percent residual sugar. The "extra dry" label came along when English champagne drinkers demanded a champagne drier than "dry." As tastes continued to move toward drier and lighter champagnes, the producers reduced the amount of sugar in the *dosage* and called the champagne Brut, which in French translates roughly as "unaltered." A small dosage was still needed to take the rough edges off of the wine, however. Finally, in recent years, the producers have become able to make a balanced truly dry champagne and the drinking public has begun to accept it as a food wine.

History of Champagne

Tradition has it that sparkling wine was invented by Dom Pérignon, a monk and winemaker at the Abbey of Hautvillers, near Épernay in the Champagne district. While developing many of the innovative techniques associated with champagne making, Dom Pérignon's successes in producing sparkling wine were preceded by the English and the Italians. Dom Pérignon's contribution was like that of a modern systems engineer—he pulled all the diverse pieces of technique together to make commercialization of sparkling wine a reality. Not the least of his integrating contributions was the melding of strong glass bottles with pressure-resisting corks, which occurred around the year 1700.

While the development of the French champagne industry was steady and consistent, that of the American industry occurred in fits and starts. Sparkling wine was first made commercially in the United States in 1842 on the Ohio River near Cincinnati by Nicholas Longworth. He used the American hybrid, Catawba, as his base wine. Another center of

sparkling winemaking started around 1865 in the Finger Lakes region of New York state. Near Hammondsport, Gold Seal and Great Western, were the first New York state producers. Both companies started out using Catawba as their base wine and continued to make sparkling wine by the *méthode champenoise* until Prohibition became law after World War I.

Another famous American champagne during the 1800s was Cook's Imperial, which was produced by the American Wine Company in St. Louis, Missouri, starting in 1858. It was also made from the Catawba grape. California's champagne industry started in Southern California, in the 1850s. This effort, which used the Mission grape, ceased in the 1880-90s due to the spread of Pierce's disease through the vineyards. The center of the California champagne industry moved to Northern California when Arpad Haraszthy started making champagne in San Francisco in 1868. He was followed by Charles Lefranc at Almaden in 1876, the Korbel brothers in 1883, and Paul Masson in 1884. Production of champagne in California, as elsewhere in the United States, ceased with Prohibition after World War I.

Following the repeal of Prohibition in 1933, most American champagne makers started into production again. Because of the high labor cost inherent in the use of the *méthode champenoise* technique, several California and New York state wineries started using the Charmat process for making sparkling wine. This process (also called the bulk process) was developed in France around 1910 by Eugène Charmat and his father, M. Maumené-Charmat. The process involves carrying out the second fermentation in a pressurized tank rather than in a bottle. This technique involves little or no aging on the lees. Soon after fermentation is complete, the sparkling wine is filtered and bottled under pressure.

Today there are dozens of producers of champagne in the United States using the traditional *méthode champenoise*. The largest producer by far is Korbel in Sonoma County, California.

Champagne and Food Pairing

Because of the delicacy of champagne's effervescence, taste and aroma, it intermingles well with the taste, texture and aroma of a wide range of foods. Brut champagne makes an excellent aperitif, while Natural goes better with the first and second courses of a meal. The sweeter champagnes go best with dessert—and, naturally, with wedding, anniversary, and birthday cake! *Blanc de Noir* champagnes, made from red grapes, have a fruitier taste and go better with heavier foods than does *Blanc de Blanc.*

The bubbles and the acidity in champagne give it the ability to match many foods and flavors that over-power still wines. Butter or margarine, eggs, creams, and purees are examples of such food ingredients. Champagne holds up to both fried and salty foods — hence its close association with caviar and other hors d'oeuvres, with salmon and trout or other fried fish, with soufflés and cream and bisque soups, and even pork sausage. These same attributes of champagne make it an excellent palate-cleanser between courses—a substitute for sorbet on occasion. Because of its high acidity, champagne can accompany spicy ethnic foods such as Szechwanese, as well as Mexican and Italian dishes.

Virginia Champagne

In Virginia, the first vintner to produce champagne was Jacques Recht, the original winemaker at Ingleside Vineyards on the Northern Neck. Ingleside has been making champagne by the *méthode champenoise* since the mid-1980s. The winery finishes the champagne in the brut style and uses Chardonnay as the *cuveé.* Another pioneer Virginia vintner making champagne by the traditional process is Dirgham Salahi, co-owner with his wife Corinne, of Oasis Vineyards. He uses a 60/40 blend of Chardonnay and Pinot Noir as his *cuveé* and ages the champagne *sur lie* (on the yeast) for two years.

Two of the newest producers of champagne in Virginia are Prince Michel Vineyards and Barboursville Vineyards. Prince Michel uses a blend of Chardonnay and Pinot Noir in its *cuveé* and leaves the champagne *sur lie* for three years before release. Luca Paschina, winemaker and general manager at Barboursville, also uses a *cuveé* of Chardonnay and Pinot Noir, but uses the Charmat process to make his sparkling wine. He does very little aging as he wants the wine to be fresh and fruity. The fifth maker of champagne in Virginia, Tom O'Grady of Rose Bower Vineyard and Winery, makes limited amounts of both dry (natural) and brut styles.

Caviar Mousse

Caviar and champagne are a traditional combination. Inexpensive and simple to prepare, this delicate mousse provides several textures and taste sensations that complement the effervescence of champagne. An imitation caviar is used in the preparation.

Makes 1 ½ cups

2 ¼ teaspoons unflavored gelatin
¼ cup dry white wine
2 hard-boiled eggs
¼ cup mayonnaise
¼ cup sour cream

1 tablespoon grated shallot
4 ounces red caviar, drained
2 teaspoons lemon juice
A pinch of white pepper
⅓ cup whipping cream

Sprinkle the gelatin over the wine in a small saucepan. Let the mixture sit for 10 minutes and then place over low heat to dissolve the gelatin. Set aside to cool.

Sieve the hard boiled eggs and gently combine them with the mayonnaise, sour cream, shallot, caviar and lemon juice. Add the gelatin mixture and blend to combine ingredients. Add pepper, seasoning to taste. Whip the cream until stiff and gently fold it into the caviar mixture.

Lightly oil a 1 ½ cup decorative mold. Spoon the caviar mixture into the mold and chill for at least 4 hours. Quickly dip mold into hot water and unmold onto a bed of lettuce leaves arranged on a platter. Serve with toast points or crackers.

Smoked Salmon Mousse in Belgian Endive

In this hors d'oeuvre the smoky flavor and slight bitterness of the Smoked Salmon Mouse with the Belgian Endives is an ideal pairing with Brut Champagne.

Serves 6

8 ounces cream cheese, at room temperature
4 ounces smoked salmon
Few drops lemon juice

3 tablespoons whipping cream
4 heads Belgian endive, pulled apart
   into petals

Combine the cream cheese, smoked salmon, lemon juice, cream, and pepper in the bowl of a food processor and blend until the mixture is smooth. Chill for at least 30 minutes. Spread some of the mousse onto each endive leaf.

Crab Stuffed Mushrooms

Select large firm mushrooms for stuffing. The thick white sauce adds richness to the filling. Use enough sauce, however, to bind the ingredients together lightly. Because mushrooms extrude moisture when cooking, an overabundance of sauce can make the hors d'oeuvres too soggy.

Serves 4 to 6

16 large mushrooms
8 ounces fresh crab meat, or
    1 can (7 ½ ounces) crab meat
2 teaspoons chopped chives
1 tablespoon semisweet Sherry
1 teaspoon Worcestershire sauce
¼ teaspoon salt

Dash of white pepper
2 tablespoons butter
1 ½ tablespoon flour
⅓ to ½ cup milk
⅓ cup grated Parmesan cheese
Paprika

Remove the stems from the mushrooms. Wipe the caps with a damp cloth or clean under running water with a brush and then dry the mushrooms with a cloth.

Pick over the crab meat to remove any cartilage and break up any large pieces. Combine crab meat, chives, sherry, Worcestershire sauce, salt, and pepper. In a small saucepan melt the butter, add flour, and mix well. Slowly add the milk, salt, and pepper. Cook, stirring over medium heat until thickened. Add the sauce by tablespoons to the crab meat, adding only enough to bind the mixture lightly. Fill the mushroom caps with the crab meat.

Place the caps in a 9 x 13-inch glass baking dish and sprinkle them with grated Parmesan cheese and paprika. Bake in a preheated 350° F. oven for 10 to 12 minutes or until bubbly.

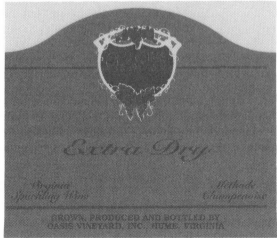

Sausage Rolls

These sausage rolls are best served with either a champagne mustard, or a hot sweet mustard and accompanied by a glass of champagne.

Serves 8

1 pound commercial puff pastry, from the freezer section of the grocery

12 small, skinless breakfast sausages
1 to 2 eggs, beaten

Roll half of the puff pastry into a rectangle measuring, 3 by 12 inches. Place 6 of the sausages along the wide edge and roll up. (You might want to place the puff pastry on a piece of waxed paper and use the paper to help you roll.)

Cut the roll into 2-inch diagonal pieces. Place each piece, seam side down, on an ungreased cookie sheet and brush with beaten egg.

Repeat with the other half of the puff pastry and the rest of the sausages. Bake sausage rolls in a preheated 375° F. oven for 8 to 10 minutes or until they are nicely browned.

Zucchini Frittata

This Zucchini Frittata may be cut into 2-inch squares and served as an hors d'oeuvre with a glass of Champagne. The Frittata may also be served as a vegetable accompaniment with a main course or as a luncheon entrée.

Serves 12 to 16 as hors d'oeuvres

5 eggs
¼ cup olive oil
¼ cup all-purpose flour
1 teaspoon baking soda
1 teaspoon baking powder

1 cup grated Cheddar cheese
½ cup grated Parmesan cheese
1 medium onion, chopped
6 cups sliced zucchini

Grease and lightly flour a 9 x 13-inch baking dish. Mix all of the ingredients except the zucchini together in a bowl. Then add the zucchini and pour the mixture into the prepared pan, spreading it evenly. Bake in preheated 350 degree F. oven for 25 minutes or until golden brown. Serve warm or at room temperature.

Mushrooms in Tarragon-Cream Sauce

These mushrooms in puff pastry shells are an elegant first course to serve with a Brut Champagne. Puff pastry shells are readily available in the frozen food section of the supermarket.

Serves 4

4 tablespoons butter of margarine
½ pound shiitake mushrooms, sliced
½ pound cremini (brown) mushrooms, sliced
½ cup dry white wine

½ cup whipping cream
3 tablespoons finely chopped fresh tarragon
Salt and pepper, to taste
4 puff pastry shells

Melt the butter in a large sauté pan. Add the mushrooms and cook until all of the liquid has evaporated and the mushrooms begin to brown lightly. Add the wine and cream and cook over medium heat until the sauce coats a spoon, about 3 to 4 minutes. Add the tarragon and salt and pepper to taste. Simmer a few more minutes to blend the flavors and serve hot in warm puff pastry shells.

Fillet Of Tuna

In this recipe, fillets of fresh tuna are marinated in white wine, lemon and cayenne pepper. They are then baked and served with a sauce of the marinade. Serve with a Brut Champagne.

Serves 6

6 tuna fillets, 6 to 8 ounces each
1 large lemon
1 cup semi-sweet white wine

¼ teaspoon cayenne pepper
2 tablespoons plain yogurt

Rinse the tuna fillets, pat them dry, and place them on a deep platter. Squeeze the lemon juice over both sides of the fish. Combine the wine and cayenne pepper, and pour over the fillets. Cover and let them stand for 20 minutes.

Place the tuna in a shallow baking dish, reserving the marinade. Bake in a preheated 350° F. oven for about 10 minutes; fillets should be rare to medium. If more doneness is desired bake them a few minutes longer, but do not overcook the fillets or they will dry out.

While the fish is baking, boil the marinade over medium-high heat, reducing its volume by one-third. Remove from heat. When the tuna is done, place the fillets on a warm platter. Add the yogurt to the marinade, heat through, and pour over the tuna.

Scallops Mediterranean Style

Fresh mushrooms, tomatoes, garlic, champagne, herbs, and avocado are combined in this recipe with lightly sautéed scallops and served on a bed of rice. The dish needs only a seasonal salad to round out the main course.

Serves 6

6 tablespoons unsalted butter
2 tablespoons minced onion
1 cup fresh tomato, seeded and finely chopped
¼ teaspoon dried thyme, crumbled
½ cup minced fresh mushrooms
2 pounds fresh scallops, well dried (large
    sea scallops should be quartered)
½ cup all-purpose flour

2 tablespoons olive oil
½ teaspoon salt
¼ teaspoon white pepper
1 ½ teaspoons very finely chopped garlic
¾ cup dry white wine
2 tablespoon parsley, finely chopped
1 avocado, peeled and cut into 1/4 inch dice
Cooked plain rice

Melt 2 tablespoons of the butter in a small skillet. Add the onion, tomato, thyme, and mushrooms, and sauté for a few minutes. Remove from heat and set aside.

Roll the well-dried scallops in flour and shake off the excess. Heat the remaining 4 tablespoons of butter and the olive oil in a very large skillet (use 2 skillets if necessary). Add the scallops and sauté for about 2 minutes, turning to brown lightly on all sides. Season with salt and pepper. Add the garlic and sauté for a few more seconds. Add the wine and the sautéed vegetables. Simmer for 2 minutes. Stir in the parsley and avocado just before serving over cooked rice.

Warm Lobster Salad

Warm salads have only recently become fashionable in this country, although they are regularly on menus in France. Shrimps, lobster, crayfish, chicken livers, small pieces of chicken or sweetbreads may be served in a warm salad. Simply sauté any of these main ingredients, some of which may have been precooked, and serve on lettuce greens. A reduced warm dressing consisting of pan juices, wine, and a little lemon juice is the accompaniment. This salad will also serve 4 as a luncheon entree. Accompany with a glass of Brut Champagne.

Serves 6

2 heads Butter lettuce	1 bay leaf
1 head red leaf lettuce	1 teaspoon white peppercorns
1 head curly endive	1 teaspoon salt
1 ripe avocado sliced	2 live lobsters (about 2 ½ pounds each)
12 cherry tomatoes, quartered	4 tablespoons butter
1 tablespoon plus 1 to 2 teaspoons lemon juice	1 cup champagne
	Salt and white pepper, to taste
2 lemons, cut in half	1 to 2 teaspoons lemon juice

Wash and dry the lettuces and curly endive and arrange them on 6 large salad plates. Arrange the avocado slices and tomatoes around the outside of the lettuce. Lightly sprinkle 1 tablespoon of lemon juice on the avocado slices to keep them from turning color. Refrigerate the salad plates, while preparing the lobsters.

Squeeze the juice of the two halved lemons into 1 ½ gallons boiling water and then add the lemon halves. Add the bay leaf, white peppercorns, and salt. Plunge the lobsters, head first, into the water and boil for 5 minutes. Then plunge them into ice water to stop the cooking. If they are not completely cooked, they will finish cooking later. Remove the tail and the claw meat. Slice the tail meat.

In a medium frying pan, melt the 4 tablespoons of butter over high heat. Sauté the lobster pieces long enough to heat through and finish cooking, if necessary. Remove the lobster to a warm dish, leaving the butter in the pan.

Add the champagne to the pan and heat to boiling over high heat. Reduce the liquid slightly and add 1 to 2 teaspoons lemon juice and salt and pepper to taste.

Quickly place the lobster in the center of each salad and pour a little sauce over each. Serve immediately.

Glazed Cornish Game Hens

This preparation of Cornish Game hens is enticing to the eye as well as to the palate. Filled with a nutty stuffing, the hens are roasted and served with a mandarin-cherry sauce. Fresh mandarins may be used when available and canned cherries may be substituted for fresh ones in the glaze. Serve with Brut Champagne.

Serves 2

2 Rock Cornish Game hens
2 small sweet potatoes, scrubbed and pierced
 for baking
½ cup pecan pieces

1 small can (11 ounces) mandarin orange
 segments in light syrup
2 tablespoons butter, melted
Salt and pepper, to taste

Remove the insides of the Cornish Game hens, rinse them, and pat them dry.

Microwave the sweet potatoes on high for about 5 to 7 minutes or until just done, but firm; or cook the sweet potatoes in their skins until just tender, about 20 minutes. Set them aside to cool.

Drain the mandarin oranges, reserving the syrup for the glaze. Peel the sweet potatoes, cut them into ½-inch cubes, and place in a mixing bowl. Add ½ cup of the orange segments, the pecans, and the melted butter. Toss gently and stuff the hens with this mixture.

Sprinkle the hens with salt and pepper and place them in a baking pan. Roast in a preheated 350° F. oven for approximately 1 hour or until done. During the last 10 minutes of baking, spoon the hens with some of the liquid from the Fruit Glaze (recipe follows), without any of the fruit. When the hens are almost done add the remaining orange segments and the cherries to the glaze and heat.

To serve, place the hens on a serving platter, spoon some of the Fruit Glaze over them, and serve the rest of the sauce on the side.

Fruit Glaze

Fresh orange juice
1 tablespoon light brown sugar
1 tablespoon cornstarch

½ cup fresh or canned Bing cherries,
    pitted and halved

While the hens are cooking, add enough fresh orange juice to the reserved mandarin syrup to make 1 cup of liquid. Place in a small saucepan and whisk in the sugar and cornstarch. Cook over medium heat, stirring constantly, until thickened. Set aside. Use some of the glaze to baste the hens, and the rest for the sauce.

Sautéed Chicken Breast with Champagne Cream Sauce

This elegant chicken dish, served on a bed of spinach, can be prepared in less than thirty minutes. A smooth velvety cream sauce flavored with tarragon is served over the chicken. Small red potatoes or wild rice and a green vegetable complete the main course.

Serves 10

5 tablespoons butter
⅛ teaspoon salt
Dash of white pepper
5 chicken breasts, split, boned and skinned
½ cup champagne (dry white wine
    may be substituted)
Steamed Spinach (recipe follows)

1 tablespoon chopped shallots
12 sprigs fresh tarragon, each
    approximately 3 inches long
Dashes of cayenne pepper and nutmeg
1 cup whipping cream
1 tablespoon butter, chilled

Melt 4 tablespoons of the butter in a large skillet. Lightly sprinkle salt and white pepper over the chicken breasts and sauté on medium-high heat until chicken is golden on both sides. Pour the champagne over the chicken and lay 1 sprig of fresh tarragon atop the side of the breast that was next to the skin. Cover the pan, turn heat to medium-low, and cook until the chicken breasts are done, about 5 minutes. While the chicken is cooking, prepare the Steamed Spinach.

Remove the chicken breasts to a warm platter, Pour out all pan juices and save. Add the remaining tablespoon of butter to the skillet and in it sauté the shallots until translucent. Add the reserved pan juices, the remaining tarragon, dashes of cayenne pepper and of nutmeg, and reduce the liquid to ¼ cup. Add the cream and continue cooking until the cream thickens and is reduced by half. Whisk in the tablespoon of chilled butter. Serve chicken breasts atop Steamed Spinach, with sauce poured over each serving.

Steamed Spinach

1 cup lightly salted water
Dash of nutmeg
2 tablespoons butter

4 bunches spinach, washed and
    stems removed

Bring the salted water to a boil in a large saucepan. Add the nutmeg and butter, and then the spinach. Cover and steam for 3 to 5 minutes, stirring halfway through the cooking process. Do not overcook the spinach. Drain well, in order not to have any of the cooking liquid on the plates.

Choucroute in Champagne with Smoked Pork Chops

Choucroute is the French word for sauerkraut, which in this recipe is cooked in champagne. Juniper berries, bacon, and tart apples are added to the sauerkraut, which surrounds smoked pork chops. This dish originated in Alsace where smoked pork is often served accompanied by a sparkling wine.

Serves 6

4 pounds sauerkraut
¼ pound bacon, chopped
2 large onions, chopped (about 4 cups)
2 large tart apples, peeled, cored and chopped
10 whole juniper berries
2 teaspoons caraway seeds

1 large bay leaf
1 ½ teaspoons freshly ground black pepper
1 bottle Brut champagne
6 smoked loin pork chops, cut ¾-inch thick
Boiled potatoes tossed with butter and
    chopped parsley

Place the sauerkraut in a colander and rinse well under cold running water. Drain well and squeeze dry.

In a large, 6 quart heavy ovenproof casserole or Dutch oven with a tight fitting lid, sauté the bacon until the fat is almost rendered, about 5 to 8 minutes over medium high heat. Add the onions, lower the heat to medium and sauté for about 15 minutes, stirring often until the onions are limp and golden in color. Stir in the sauerkraut, apples, juniper berries, caraway seeds, bay leaf, pepper and champagne, mixing well. Cover the casserole and bake in a preheated 350° F. oven for 1 ½ hours, stirring about every 30 minutes.

VIRGINIA

1814 Barboursville Ruins · Virginia Historic Landmark

BARBOURSVILLE
BRUT
Natural Sparkling Wine

PRODUCED AND BOTTLED BY BARBOURSVILLE VINEYARDS, BARBOURSVILLE, VA. ALC. 12% BY VOL.

Remove the casserole from the oven and spoon half of the sauerkraut into a bowl. Arrange the pork chops, in a single layer if possible, over the top of the sauerkraut in the casserole. Cover with the sauerkraut in the bowl. Return to the oven and bake, uncovered, for 30 minutes. Sauerkraut should be moist, but not soupy. Serve with boiled potatoes that have been drizzled with melted butter, then tossed with chopped parsley.

Orange Soufflé with Strawberry-Rhubarb Sauce

Soufflés are special. They are as light as air and are considered by many to be the finest of the French-inspired desserts. The basis of a dessert soufflé is either a custard sauce or a fruit puree to which beaten egg whites have been added. Soufflés cannot be hurried in preparation or baking time, but they must be served immediately when they are ready. Frozen rhubarb and strawberries may be used when fresh fruit is not in season. This special dessert calls for a glass of champagne.

Serves 6

Strawberry-Rhubarb Sauce

1 rib rhubarb, peeled and diced, about ¾ cup   1 cup orange juice
¼ cup sugar   8 to 10 fresh strawberries

Place the rhubarb, the 1/4 cup of sugar and the orange juice in a saucepan and bring to a boil. Reduce the heat and simmer until the sauce is reduced to 2/3 cup, about 15 to 20 minutes. Remove from heat and set aside. Ten minutes before the soufflé is done, add the strawberries to the rhubarb sauce and cook gently over medium low heat.

Soufflé

12 ounces cream cheese, softened
3 egg yolks, room temperature
5 tablespoon sugar
¼ cup Cointreau
1 teaspoon grated orange zest

¼ teaspoon ground cardamom
½ piece vanilla bean, 2 to 3 inches long
4 egg whites, room temperature
Pinch of salt
1 teaspoon orange juice

Preheat the oven to 350° F. Butter and lightly sprinkle with sugar a 1 ½-quart soufflé dish. In a food processor, mix the cream cheese, egg yolks, sugar, Cointreau, orange zest, cardamom and the seeds of the vanilla bean. Process until smooth and completely blended. Pour mixture into a large bowl and set aside.

In a large mixing bowl, beat the egg whites with a pinch of salt until soft peaks form. Add the orange juice and continue beating until stiff.

Add one-third of the egg whites to the cream cheese mixture and blend well. Carefully fold in the remaining egg whites only until blended. Pour the mixture into the prepared soufflé dish. After gently leveling the top of the soufflé, make a shallow groove by running a knife around the top about 1 inch in from the edge. Bake in a preheated 350° F. oven for about 30 minutes or until the top is golden. As soon as it is done, serve the soufflé with the hot sauce.

Souffléd Eggs

In this brunch dish, the eggs are first poached and then baked in a very light cheese soufflé mixture.

Serves 4

3 tablespoons butter
⅓ cup flour
2 cups boiling milk
3 egg yolks
3 ounces Swiss cheese, grated

2 ounces Parmesan cheese, grated
5 egg whites, at room temperature
Salt and white pepper, to taste
8 poached eggs

Melt the butter in a medium saucepan over medium heat. Add the flour and stir a few minutes, making a roux. Add the hot milk, stirring vigorously. Reduce the heat to low and let the mixture simmer for 10 minutes, then remove it from the heat. In a small bowl lightly beat the egg yolks, then add a little of the hot milk mixture and mix to incorporate. Then slowly add the yolks to the pan with the milk mixture. Mix well. Stir in the cheeses, a little at a time until they are melted. Transfer the mixture to a bowl and let it cool to room temperature.

Add a pinch of salt to the egg whites and beat them until medium-stiff peaks form. Fold the egg whites, ⅓rd at a time, into the cheese mixture.

Spread a quarter of the souffle mixture on the bottom of a 9 by 13 -inch flat casserole dish. Bake for 10 minutes in a preheated 400° F. oven. Remove from the oven and lay the poached eggs on top in a pattern that will make serving easy. Spread the remaining souffle mixture over the eggs and return the casserole to the oven. Bake until puffed and golden brown, about 15 to 20 minutes. Serve immediately.

Pithiviers with Ham And Spinach

Pithiviers, pronounced pit-o-vey, is a dessert tart of puff pastry that is normally filled with almond cream. It is a specialty of the town of Pithiviers, forty miles south of Paris. Filled with ham, chard and cheese, this version makes a delectable brunch entree that may be made ahead. A glass of champagne pairs well with this unique dish.

Serves 6

1 bunch spinach, cleaned
½ pound cooked ham, diced
   (about 1 ½ cups)
4 ounces tangy goat cheese, crumbled
3 whole green onions, finely sliced

¼ teaspoon freshly ground pepper
3 large eggs
1 ¼ pounds puff pastry, or 1 package
   (17 ¼ ounces) frozen puff pastry sheets

Steam spinach until tender. Cool and squeeze dry. There should be about 1 cup. Chop the spinach finely and combine it with the ham, cheese, onions, pepper, and 2 beaten eggs. Mix well.

Roll puff pastry ¼ inch thick. (Pre-rolled sheets can be used as they are.(Cut our two pastry circles, each 9 inches in diameter. Place 1 on a cookie sheet and spread the spinach filling evenly in the center, leaving an inch uncovered all around the edge. Beat the remaining egg and brush the uncovered part with some of the egg wash. Top with the second pastry circle and seal it all the way around. Using the blunt-sided tip of a knife, pull the pastry edge in about ½ inch at 1-inch intervals to create a scalloped edge all around. Brush the tart with beaten egg. Cut a ½-inch-round vent hole in the center and, using the point of a knife, make a pattern of spiral lines from the edges toward the center, cutting into the dough about 1⁄16 of an inch.

Refrigerate the tart for at least 2 hours. Bake in a preheated 375° F. oven for about 30 minutes, or until puffed and golden brown.

RED WINES

Baco Noir

This red French hybrid was developed around the turn of the century, and was the first French hybrid brought to the United States after World War II. Baco Noir's French parent is a high-acid white varietal, called Folle Blanche, which had been popular in the Cognac region of France at the time Baco Noir was developed. It's American lineage stems from Vitis Riparia, *a less "foxy" species of native American grapes than the* Vitis Labrusca. *The grape has proven only moderately resistant to frost.*

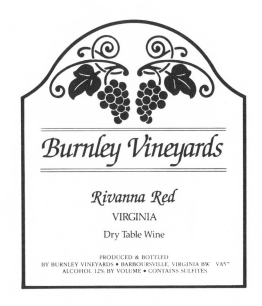

Baco Noir has not been generally popular in Virginia with only one winery making it into a wine, Mountain Cove Vineyards. Al Weed at Mountain Cove uses Baco Noir as the primary wine in his Harvest Red. Al leaves the juice from the Baco Noir grapes on the skins for ten days and then, after fermenting it in steel tanks, ages the wine in oak barrels for eight months. Wine made from Baco Noir in Virginia is full-bodied and has a recognizable bouquet. Lee Reeder, winemaker at Burnley, uses Baco Noir as a blending wine, along with several other French hybrids, in his Rivanna Red table wine.

Piquant Vermicelli

This pasta dish is a delightful combination of flavors—Canadian bacon, green onions, mushrooms, capers, and toasted pine nuts—in a light cream sauce. The smoky flavor of the bacon and the tartness of the capers are enhanced by a light red wine, such as a Baco Noir.

Serves 4

2 tablespoons olive oil
½ pound crimini (brown) mushrooms, sliced
¼ pound shiitake mushrooms, sliced
1 (6 ounce) package Canadian bacon, julienned
4 green onions, chopped

2 heaping teaspoons drained capers
8 ounces vermicelli, cooked al dente
½ cup Parmesan cheese
¾ cup whipping cream
¼ cup toasted pine nuts
Additional Parmesan cheese, if desired

Heat the oil in a large skillet over medium heat. Add the mushrooms and sauté until they are tender and slightly browned, about 10 minutes. Then add the Canadian bacon, onions, and capers and heat through. Add the vermicelli, cheese, cream, and pine nuts. Toss to combine the ingredients. Continue cooking until the sauce begins to thicken and coats the pasta, and the mixture is heated through. Serve immediately and top with additional Parmesan cheese, if desired.

Fried Chicken

There are many versions of fried chicken. Some cooks only flour the chicken; others use a combination of flour and cornmeal, while others dip the chicken pieces in milk or cream before breading. The chicken may be served with either a cream gravy made with the pan drippings or plain. This version of fried chicken includes some spices for extra flavoring.

Serves 4

1 chicken (3 and ½ to 4 pounds), cut into serving pieces
1 can (6 ounces) evaporated milk
⅓ cup all-purpose flour
⅓ cup cornmeal
½ cup cornflake crumbs
¼ teaspoon salt

¼ teaspoon pepper
¼ teaspoon garlic powder
¾ teaspoon dried thyme
Paprika
2 tablespoons margarine
3 tablespoons solid vegetable shortening

Rinse the chicken pieces and dry them. Place the evaporated milk in a bowl or soup plate. Combine the flour, cornmeal, cornflake crumbs, salt, pepper, garlic powder, and thyme on a piece of waxed paper. Dip each piece of chicken in the milk and then roll it in the flour combination, coating it well on all sides. Then sprinkle each piece with paprika.

Melt the shortening and butter in a large skillet over medium heat. Add the chicken pieces, paprika side down, and brown them, about 8 minutes. Sprinkle the top side with paprika, turn, and brown the other side. Cover the skillet and continue cooking over medium-low heat for 15 minutes. Turn the chicken and cook another 20 minutes, or until done, turning the chicken once. Serve chicken with the following gravy, if desired.

Gravy

2 tablespoons flour
1 ½ cups half-and-half

Salt and pepper, to taste

Pour off all except 3 tablespoons of the fat in the frying pan. Stir in the flour and cook for a few minutes. Pour in the half-and-half and cook, stirring constantly, until the sauce is smooth and thick. Season to taste with salt and pepper. Serve with the chicken.

Barbera

Barbera is one of the world's most widely planted grapes. Native to Italy, where it is the most commonly planted red grape, Barbera is also widely planted in the San Joaquin Valley of California. While many Italians consider it an everyday wine, Barbera is made into an excellent one in the cooler climates of the Piedmont region of Italy. The wine has a deep purplish hue, is generally high in acid, and has a full fruity character. Usually containing moderate tannins, Barbera is best enjoyed while young, although the best vintages from the Piedmont region have required some aging to be fully appreciated.

Barboursville Vineyards is the only grower and producer of Barbera wine in Virginia. Luca Paschina, the General Manager and winemaker at Barboursville, is from the Piedmont region of Italy and has a special affection for this comfortable wine. To produce a fruity wine that can be enjoyed almost immediately after a short aging period, Paschina ferments the juice in an Italian-developed rotating fermentor. This space capsule-like fermentor treats the grapes gently as it rotates briefly every hour or so, thereby minimizing the amount of harsh tannins imparted to the wine.

Vegetarian Lasagna

This Vegetarian Lasagna recipe utilizes a variety of vegetables and others may be substituted, if desired. The use of cottage cheese instead of the traditional ricotta makes the dish lighter. The lasagna may be prepared ahead and baked before dinner. Any leftovers may be warmed in a microwave oven.

Serves 6 to 8

1 (16 ounce) can tomatoes, chopped and juice reserved
3 (6 ounce) cans tomato sauce
¾ teaspoon dried oregano, crumbled
1 teaspoon dried basil leaves, crumbled
¼ teaspoon pepper
2 tablespoons olive oil
1 medium onion, chopped
1 clove garlic, minced
2 medium zucchini, cut into small cubes
8 ounces mushrooms, sliced (white and brown mixed, if available)

1 medium carrot, chopped
½ green pepper, chopped
½ red pepper, chopped
1 cup (4 ounces) shredded mozzarella cheese
2 cups low-fat cottage cheese
⅓ cup grated Parmesan cheese
⅓ cup chopped fresh basil leaves or parsley
8 ounces lasagna noodles, cooked, rinsed and drained
Parmesan cheese, for garnish

Combine the tomatoes, their juice, tomato sauce, dried oregano, dried basil, and pepper in a medium saucepan and simmer over low heat for 15 minutes. Heat the oil in a large skillet over medium heat and add the onion, garlic, zucchini, mushrooms, carrot, and peppers. Sauté the vegetables until barely tender about 7 minutes. Then combine them with the sauce and simmer for a few minutes.

In a bowl combine the mozzarella, cottage, and Parmesan cheeses. Add the fresh basil or parsley.

Thinly cover the bottom of a lasagna casserole or a 12 x 8-inch casserole with some of the sauce. Place a layer of noodles over the sauce. Top with half of the cheese mixture and half of the remaining sauce. Repeat the layer of noodles, cheese, and sauce. Sprinkle additional Parmesan cheese on top. Bake in a preheated 350° F. oven for 45 to 50 minutes or until bubbly. If refrigerated before cooking, let casserole come to room temperature and increase cooking time by 10 minutes.

Penne with Peppers and Sausage

Its fun to have a pasta party and serve several different pastas. This is a typical northern Italian recipe for pasta. Serve this dish with a glass of Barbera, a Virginia wine made from an Italian grape.

Serves 4 as an entrée or 8 at a pasta party

1 large clove garlic, peeled and cut in half
3 tablespoons olive oil
½ medium onion, chopped
1 large red pepper, diced
1 large yellow pepper, diced
1 (28 ounce) can Italian plum tomatoes with juice, coarsely chopped and mixed with 1 cup water

½ teaspoon salt
½ teaspoon freshly ground pepper
Pinch of red pepper flaked
4 mild Italian sausages, casings removed and crumbled
⅔ cup freshly grated Parmesan cheese
1 pound ridged penne pasta

Sauté the garlic in the olive oil in a large saucepan over medium heat until browned. Discard the garlic and add the onions and peppers to the pan. Sauté for about 7 minutes or until the onion is wilted. Add the tomatoes, salt, pepper, and red pepper flakes and cook for 10 minutes over medium heat.

Place the sausage meat in another skillet with 1/4 cup water. Cook the sausage over medium heat until it is lightly browned and the water has evaporated. Add the sausage meat along with 3 tablespoons of its fat to the sauce mixture. Cook over medium heat for 10 minutes.

While the sauce is cooking, boil the pasta until it is al dente. Drain the penne well and transfer it to a warm platter. Add the sauce and Parmesan cheese. Toss thoroughly and serve at once.

Linguine with Salmon Sauce

The richness of the salmon and the cream sauce in this pasta recipe makes it an ideal dish to serve with a light red wine such as Barbera. Combine this and the previous penne recipe for an interesting pasta party.

Serves 4 as an entrée or 8 at a pasta party

6 tablespoons unsalted butter
1 clove garlic, peeled and cut in half
½ cup chopped red onion
½ cup small cubes of prosciutto
¾ pound fresh salmon filet, cut
    into 1-inch cubes
3 teaspoons chopped fresh parsley
2 tablespoons chopped fresh basil

2 cups canned Italian tomatoes with juice,
    tomatoes chopped
¼ teaspoon salt
½ teaspoon freshly ground black pepper
½ tablespoon extra virgin olive oil
½ cup whipping cream
1 pound linguine

Melt 4 tablespoons of the butter in a large saucepan over medium heat and add the garlic, sautéing it until brown. Discard the garlic and add the onions, prosciutto, and salmon, separating the salmon pieces with a fork as they cook. Continue cooking for 3 minutes. Then add the parsley, basil, tomatoes, salt, pepper, and olive oil and stir gently to combine. Simmer the sauce, uncovered, for 10 minutes. Then add the cream and simmer for another 5 minutes.

While the sauce is simmering, cook the pasta until it is al dente. Drain the linguine and place it on a large warm platter. Add the sauce and the remaining 2 tablespoons of butter. Toss and serve immediately.

Roasted Pheasant

At one time wild pheasants were hunted in the woods of Virginia. Now they are available in gourmet stores. In this recipe the pheasant breast is covered with bacon to provide additional moisture during roasting. The juniper-flavored cabbage is a good flavor contrast to the tarragon and slightly sweet glaze of the pheasant.

Serves 2

1 pheasant (2 to 2 ½ pounds)
⅓ pound sausage
½ tart apple, peeled, cored and chopped
2 tablespoons chopped onion
3 large mushrooms, chopped
¼ cup golden raisins
¼ cup chopped walnuts
¼ cup chopped parsley

1 egg, beaten
½ teaspoon celery seeds
Salt and pepper, to taste
1 large sprig fresh tarragon or
    1 teaspoon dried tarragon
3 slices bacon
½ cup dry sherry
2 tablespoons red currant jelly

Rinse the pheasant and pat it dry. Combine the sausage, apple, celery, mushrooms, raisins, walnuts, parsley, egg, celery seeds, salt, and pepper. Stuff the bird with the sausage mixture.

Place the pheasant in a shallow roasting pan. Put the tarragon sprig on the breast of the bird or sprinkle it with dried tarragon. Then place the bacon slices over the breast and roast the bird in a preheated 350° F. oven for 1 hour, or until the bird is almost tender. Pour off the fat. Combine the sherry and jelly, mixing well to blend. Baste the bird several times with this glaze and continue roasting it for another 15 minutes, or until the pheasant is tender.

To serve, spoon some cabbage on each of two plates. Cut the pheasant in half and place each half on top of the cabbage.

Savory Cabbage with Juniper Berries

½ medium head savory cabbage
2 tablespoons butter
⅓ cup chopped onion
10 juniper berries, slightly crushed

¼ cup chicken broth
¼ cup white wine
Salt and pepper, to taste

Shred the cabbage. Melt the butter in a medium-size saucepan, add the onions, and sauté them until they are a light brown. Add the rest of the ingredients. Cover and bring to a boil, then cook over low heat for 15 to 20 minutes, or until the cabbage is done.

Cabernet Franc

Until recently, Cabernet France has suffered in the shadow of the revered Cabernet Sauvignon. The two Cabernets have much in common, although the Franc tends to have less tannins and acid. Consequently, it can be enjoyed when still young, while its brother is best appreciated after being aged for 5 to 15 years. In the Bordeaux region of France where they both originated, Franc is traditionally used as a blending wine with Cabernet Sauvignon to lessen the latter's harshness. In the more northerly Loire region, however, Franc stands alone as a light red or rosé wine. There it has a light body and high acidity and is enjoyed when newly bottled.

Franc has become increasingly popular in Virginia in recent years. Virginia's climate is apparently very suitable to the Franc vines. There are currently seven wineries offering Cabernet Franc wines, but the list is growing as there are 19 wineries plus other growers cultivating this variety. The current six are: Barboursville Vineyards, Horton Vineyards, Jefferson (previously Simeon) Vineyards, Oasis Vineyard, Tarara Vineyard and Winery, Villa Appalaccia, and Willowcroft.

Luca Paschina at Barboursville ferments his Cabernet Franc in a rotating fermentor and then ages it in oak for four months before bottling. Dennis Horton at Horton and David Collins at Willowcroft blend a modest amount of Cabernet Sauvignon with their Cabernet Franc to give the wine more body and complexity. Horton also adds a touch of Norton wine to the blend. The winemaker at Tarara, Debbie Dellinger, makes a white wine from Cabernet France, which she has labeled Blanc de Cabernet Franc, while Dirgham Salahi at Oasis bottles a blush wine made from Franc, which he calls Dogwood Pink.

Beef Stroganoff

The greater the variety of mushrooms used in this dish of Russian origin, the better the flavor. Beef Stroganoff is traditionally served over lightly buttered noodles and is complemented by a full-bodied red wine, such as a Cabernet Franc.

Serves 4

2 tablespoons vegetable oil
1 ½ pounds beef filet, sliced ½-inch thick
    and cut into ½-inch thick strips
2 tablespoons butter
¼ cup finely chopped shallots
1 ounce brandy

4 tablespoons paprika
2 cups mushrooms, quartered(white domestic, brown, shiitake, and oyster mushrooms)
¾ cup whipping cream
½ cup sour cream
Salt and freshly ground pepper, to taste

In a large heavy skillet, heat the oil over medium-high heat. Add the meat and sear it quickly. The meat should be medium rare in the center. Remove the meat to a warm platter.

In another skillet, heat the butter over medium-high heat and sauté the shallots until they are soft. Add the mushrooms and sauté for 3 to 4 minutes. Lower the heat to medium and add the brandy and paprika. Cook for another minute. Then add the cream and sour cream, stirring to blend. Cook until heated through. Then add the meat and cook again until heated. Season to taste with salt and pepper. Serve with noodles.

Spaghetti Sauce

This piquant spaghetti sauce is made with beef and mild Italian sausage and seasoned with all of the traditional spices. Serve this pasta dish with a hearty red wine, such as Cabernet Franc.

Serves 6

3 tablespoons olive oil
1 large onion, chopped
2 large garlic cloves, minced
1 ½ pounds lean ground beef
2 mild Italian sausages, casings removed
    and broken into small pieces
½ pound mushrooms, sliced
1 medium green pepper, diced
2 cans (1 pound each) tomatoes, chopped
2 cans (8 ounces each) tomato sauce
1 can (6 ounces) tomato paste

½ teaspoon salt
½ teaspoon pepper
⅓ cup fresh chopped basil or
    2 teaspoons dried basil
3 tablespoons fresh chopped oregano or
    1 teaspoon dried oregano
3 tablespoons fresh chopped thyme or
    1 ½ teaspoons dried thyme
1 ¼ pounds spaghetti, cooked al dente
Freshly grated Parmesan cheese

Heat the olive oil in a large Dutch oven, add the onions and garlic, and sauté until limp and very lightly browned. Add the beef and sausage meat and sauté until the meat loses its pink color and is lightly browned. Mix in the mushrooms and green pepper. Then add the chopped tomatoes and their juice and the remaining ingredients. Thin the sauce with ½ cup water. Bring to a slow boil and then cook over low heat for 1 to 1 ½ hours, stirring occasionally. Remove any accumulated fat from the top of the sauce.

To serve, place the cooked spaghetti in a warm bowl. Add the sauce and toss to coat the pasta. Serve with grated Parmesan cheese.

Stuffed Crown Roast of Lamb

Lamb is often served for Easter dinner. Today, "spring lamb" has become a marketing term, since most of the lamb is slaughtered in the early fall. This Stuffed Crown Roast of Lamb makes an elegant presentation for a holiday dinner.

Serves 8

1 crown roast of lamb consisting of 14 to 16 chops

Stuffing

½ cup dark raisins
1 teaspoon grated lemon zest
1 tablespoon grated orange zest
1 tablespoon lemon juice
3 tablespoons orange juice
1 pound ground lamb
¼ cup chopped walnuts
2 tablespoons pine nuts
¾ cup coarsely chopped fresh mushrooms
1 medium onion, chopped

2 slices white bread, torn into small pieces
¼ cup finely chopped fresh parsley
1 ½ tablespoons chopped fresh rosemary
½ teaspoon ground coriander
1 egg, beaten
½ teaspoon garlic powder
Salt and pepper, to taste
6 cherry tomatoes
4 mushroom caps
4 walnut halves

Have your butcher prepare a crown roast, Frenching the bones, from two or three racks of lamb, depending on their size.

To make the stuffing, place the raisins in a bowl, add the fruit zests and juices. Allow the mixture to stand for 30 minutes. Combine the remaining stuffing ingredients in a large bowl and add the soaked raisin mixture.

Lightly coat the bottom of a roasting pan with olive oil. Season the roast with salt and pepper, place it in the pan, and spoon the stuffing in the center of the roast. Garnish the top of the stuffing with the cherry tomatoes, mushrooms, and walnuts.

Protect the ends of the bones with foil. Also put foil over the stuffing for the first 30 minutes of cooking time. Roast in a preheated 400° F. oven for 15 minutes, then reduce the oven heat to 375° F. and continue roasting for a total of 1 ¼ to 1 ½ hours, depending on the weight of the roast. A meat thermometer inserted into the meatiest part of the lamb chop should read 135° F. for pink lamb. Remove the meat from the oven and place it on a platter. To serve, cut the lamb into chops between the bones and serve with the stuffing.

Lamb Shanks with Fennel

The anise flavor of the Italian vegetable, fennel, pairs well with lamb. Serve this lamb dish with a full-bodied Cabernet Franc.

Serves 4

4 lamb shanks
Salt and pepper
2 tablespoons olive oil
1 medium onion, chopped
1 large fennel bulb, sliced lengthwise
3 ounces mushrooms, sliced
1 clove garlic, chopped

1 medium tomato, peeled and chopped
1 cup white wine
⅓ cup chicken broth
2 tablespoons chopped fresh rosemary leaves
2 tablespoons flour combined with
  ⅓ cup water

Sprinkle the lamb shanks with salt and pepper. Heat the olive oil in a large skillet which has a lid or in a Dutch oven over medium heat. Add the lamb shanks and brown them on both sides. Remove lamb shanks and add the onion, fennel, mushrooms, and garlic. Sauté for about 5 minutes or until the vegetables are limp. Add the tomato, white wine, and water and combine.

Return the lamb shanks to the pan, placing vegetables around them. Sprinkle the top of the shanks with rosemary. Cover and bake in a preheated 325° F. oven for 2 hours. Remove any accumulated fat from the pan juices and thicken with the flour and water combination.

1992
Cabernets
51% Cabernet Franc
26% Cabernet Sauvignon • 23% Merlot
VIRGINIA
DRY RED TABLE WINE

TARARA

PRODUCED & BOTTLED BY TARARA LEESBURG, VA 22075 BW-VA-76

Cabernet Sauvignon

Cabernet Sauvignon is considered by wine aficionados throughout the world as the premier red wine grape. Its greatest fame derives from being the basis of the fine wines of Bordeaux, France. While Cabernet Sauvignon makes a superb full-bodied wine by itself, vintners frequently add modest amounts of Merlot and Cabernet Franc, plus small quantities of Malbec and Petit Verdot. These additional elements add complexity to the wine and mellow the aggressive character of the Cabernet Sauvignon. The characteristic undertones of Cabernet Sauvignon are those of black currants and cedar wood.

One of the advantages of Cabernet Sauvignon is that it buds late, thereby avoiding most of the problems associated with late spring frosts. It also ripens later than most grape varieties, however, which can present problems associated with fall rains and early frosts. The grape's thick skin helps it to resist many insects and even moisture-related diseases. One of Cabernet Sauvignon's disadvantages from the vintners standpoint is that it is not a heavy producer, relative to other grape varieties

To reach its peak of enjoyment, Cabernet Sauvignon generally requires considerable aging—anywhere from two-to-fifteen years, depending on the amount of tannin in the wine. Because of its astringency, drinking Cabernet Sauvignon before its time has been described as similar to rock climbing, a "masochist's delight." Like Chardonnay, Cabernet Sauvignon has a natural affinity with oak and vintners traditionally meld the elements of fruit and wood tannins by fermenting and aging the wine in oak barrels before bottling.

Some vintners reduce the time required for aging by subjecting the grapes and juice to rapid fermentation using the macération carbonique process, which ferments the juice from inside the grapes. Another scheme, developed in Italy, is to use a space capsule-like rotating fermentor, which periodically rotates the grapes and skins.

Next to Chardonnay, Cabernet Sauvignon is the most widely planted wine grape in Virginia, with 31 vintners growing and making Cabernet Sauvignon wine. Cabernet Sauvignon's ability to grow in a wide variety of climes has made it one of the easiest to grow in Virginia's relatively hot and humid climatic conditions. Another advantage of Cabernet Sauvignon for Virginia vintners is that it buds late.

Fortunately for wine drinkers, Virginia Cabernet Sauvignon can be enjoyed while fairly young as Virginia-grown Cabernet grapes do not develop as much tannin as do those in Bordeaux. A number of Virginia vintners age their Cabernet Sauvignon in barrels for 18 to 24 months, while others bottle the wine after 12 months and then let it age in the bottle for up to 12 additional months.

Virginia vintners also vary in their practice of blending other red wines with their Cabernet Sauvignon. While several wineries produce a pure Cabernet Sauvignon wine, most vintners prefer to add a modest amount of Merlot and/or Cabernet Franc to soften the aggressive flavors of the Cabernet Sauvignon grape.

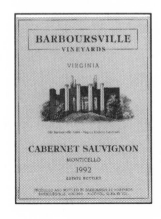

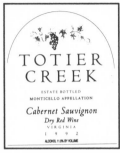

Braised Loin of Venison

The opening of deer season in the fall is always a much-awaited event in Virginia and venison is a highly prized meat. In this dish it pairs well with Cabernet Sauvignon. The combination of buttermilk and milk used in this recipe softens the gamey taste of venison and also helps tenderize the meat. If a more gamey taste is desired, omit the marinade. The red wine used in cooking aids in making the meat more tender.

Serves 4

1 loin of venison (about 1 ½ pounds)	2 tablespoons butter or margarine
¾ cup milk	1 medium onion, chopped
¾ cup buttermilk	1 slice bacon, diced
½ teaspoon salt	6 juniper berries
¼ teaspoon pepper	½ cup sliced shiitake mushrooms
¼ teaspoon dried thyme	⅓ cup finely diced carrot
¼ teaspoon dried marjoram	¾ cup red wine
¼ teaspoon dried rosemary	⅓ cup fresh cranberries
¼ teaspoon dried sage	2 tablespoons sour cream

Place the venison loin in a small, oblong bowl. Combine the milk and buttermilk and pour over the venison to just cover the meat. Cover the dish with plastic wrap and store in the refrigerator for 24 to 36 hours.

Remove the meat from the marinade and pat it dry with paper towels. Discard the marinade. Combine the salt, pepper, and spices and pat them onto the meat.

Melt the butter in a small roaster or oven-proof casserole over medium heat. Add the venison, onion, and bacon and lightly brown the meat on both sides. Add the juniper berries, mushrooms, carrot, and wine. Cover the roaster and bake in a preheated 325° F. oven for 45 minutes to 1 hour or until the meat is no longer pink on the inside.

In the meantime, cook the cranberries in a little water just until they burst. (This may be done in a microwave oven.) Remove the venison from the pan to a warm platter and keep it warm. Add the cooked cranberries to the pan juices, then add the sour cream and stir to combine. If necessary thicken the pan juices with a little flour and water combination. Slice the venison and serve with the gravy.

INGLESIDE
PLANTATION
VINEYARDS

Virginia
C a b e r n e t   S a u v i g n o n
1991

Fillet of Beef in Puff Pastry

This dish is akin to Beef Wellington, but uses a mushroom mixture instead of the traditional liver pâté. The earthy qualities of the mushrooms pair well with the beef, both of which are complemented by Cabernet Sauvignon.

Serves 4

½ ounce dried porcini mushrooms
1 sheet frozen puff pastry (from
    a 17 ¼ ounce package)
2 tablespoons olive oil
12 ounces crimini (brown) mushrooms, sliced
6 ounces shiitake mushrooms, cut in strips
1 medium onion, chopped

Salt and pepper, to taste
Flour for rolling pastry
1 ½ pounds fillet of beef
1 egg yolk, beaten
½ cup beef broth
2 tablespoons whipping cream

Put the porcini mushrooms in a bowl, pour 1 cup boiling water over them, and let them soften for at least 30 minutes. Then defrost the pastry.

While the pastry is defrosting, heat the olive oil in a large skillet over medium heat, add the crimini and shiitake mushrooms and onion, and sauté them for a few minutes. Squeeze as much liquid as possible out of the porcini mushrooms, reserve the liquid. Then cut the porcini into strips and add them to the mushrooms in the skillet. Add salt and pepper, to taste. Continue sautéing the mushrooms until all of the liquid has evaporated. Set aside and let cool while preparing the pastry.

Roll out the pastry so that it is large enough to fit around the piece of beef and long enough to generously seal the ends. Salt and pepper the beef. Place the pastry on a baking sheet. Then put a layer of mushrooms the same width as the beef down the center of the pastry. Place the beef on top of the mushrooms. Pack the remaining mushrooms on top of and around the sides of the beef, using your hands to press them onto the meat. Quickly fold the pastry across the top and brush the overlap with some of the beaten egg yolk. Then fold the ends of the roll to close it and seal it with the egg wash. If there are any pieces of dough remaining, use them to make a design on top, sticking them on with the egg wash. Brush the top of the pastry with remaining egg wash. (It may be necessary to use an additional egg yolk.)

Bake the pastry in a preheated 375° F. oven for 22 to 25 minutes for medium rare. Insert a meat thermometer to test the doneness. It should register 140° F.

While the beef is baking combine the reserved mushroom liquid and the beef broth in a small saucepan and reduce by half. Just before the beef is ready, stir in the cream and heat through.

To serve, slice the beef, divide among 4 plates, and spoon some sauce over each serving.

Pot Roast

Pot roast is an American tradition. It dates back to colonial days when whole meals were cooked in one utensil, either over an open hearth or in a brick oven. A pot roast was also a way of cooking a less tender piece of meat, hence chuck is usually designated for this dish.

Serves 6 to 8

1 (3 ½ to 4 pound) bone-in chuck roast
½ teaspoon salt
¼ teaspoon pepper
½ teaspoon garlic powder
½ teaspoon onion powder
2 tablespoons olive oil
1 cup sliced mushrooms
1 medium onion, chopped
1 (8 ounce) can tomato sauce

1 cup dry red wine
½ cup water
4 large carrots, peeled and cut into large
   chunks
6 medium red or white potatoes, halved
½ pound green beans, cut into 2-inch pieces
¾ cup fresh or thawed frozen peas
¼ cup flour blended with ½ water,
   to thicken gravy

Trim roast of any excess outside fat. Season with salt, pepper, garlic powder, and onion powder. Heat the olive oil in a large roaster or Dutch oven. Add the roast and brown it well on both sides. As the second side is browning, add the mushrooms and onion.

Combine the tomato sauce, wine, and water. When the roast is browned on both sides pour the tomato sauce mixture around the roast, lifting it so that the liquid is also underneath it. Place the carrots and potatoes around the roast. Cover the pan and place in a preheated 325° F. oven for 1 ½ hours. Then add the green beans on top of the roast and continue cooking for another 50 minutes. During the last 10 minutes of cooking time add the peas.

Remove the roast to a warm platter. Place the pan on medium-low heat and gradually add enough of the flour-water mixture to thicken the gravy. Slice the meat and serve with the vegetables and gravy.

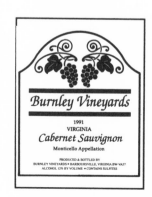

Grilled Leg of Lamb with American Ratatouille

This is a wonderful way to cook a leg of lamb well in advance of serving. The pomegranate juice can be purchased at a health food store. You can marinate the meat either in a deep bowl or in a plastic bag. The longer the meat marinates (up to 48 hours), the better the flavor. Salt and pepper should be added at serving time as salting meat before grilling tends to make it tough.

Inspired by the French vegetable dish, this American Ratatouille includes several vegetables that originated in the Americas—tomatoes, corn, and peppers. A Cabernet Sauvignon complements both the lamb and the Ratatouille.

Serves 8

1 (4 to 5 pound) leg of lamb butterflied	6 springs of rosemary
3 cloves garlic, cut in quarters	Pomegranate juice
1 large onion, sliced in rings	Red wine

Trim any fat and muscle from the pieces of lamb. Place them in a deep bowl or in a large plastic bag. Put the garlic, onion, and rosemary between the pieces of meat. Combine equal amounts of pomegranate juice and red wine to cover the meat by 1 inch. Cover the bowl with plastic wrap or seal the bag and refrigerate. Turn the meat every 24 hours.

Grill over hot coals 4 to 5 minutes per side, depending on the thickness of the meat. Then immediately place the lamb in a flat baking dish (such as a Pyrex dish) and place in a 150° F. oven. The meat may be held this way for up to 1 ½ hours and will still be pink when served.

American Ratatouille

3 small Italian eggplants, sliced 1/4-inch thick	Kernels from 4 ears of fresh corn
5 tablespoons olive oil	Salt and pepper, to taste
2 onions sliced	4 medium zucchini, sliced
1 cup sliced mushrooms	4 to 5 medium tomatoes, sliced
1 medium red pepper, chopped	½ teaspoon dried thyme
1 medium green pepper, chopped	¼ cup freshly ground Parmesan cheese
1 clove garlic, chopped	

Sprinkle the eggplant slices with salt and let them sit in a colander for 30 minutes. Then rinse and pat dry with paper towels. This process removes the bitterness from the egg plant.

Heat 3 tablespoons of the olive oil in a large skillet over medium heat. Add the onions and sauté them until wilted. Add the mushrooms, peppers, eggplants, and garlic and continue sautéing until the eggplants begin to soften. Place the mixture into a large round or oblong casserole. Add the corn, salt, and pepper.

Arrange the zucchini slices and tomato slices in alternating, overlapping rows on top of the eggplant mixture. (May be prepared ahead to this point and refrigerated.) Just before baking, sprinkle the casserole with 1 tablespoon of the olive oil and the thyme. Bake in a preheated 350° F. oven for 35 minutes. Then drizzle the remaining tablespoon of olive oil over the vegetables and sprinkle with the Parmesan cheese. Bake for another 15 minutes.

Chocolate Decadence Torte

This chocolate torte is further enriched with ground almonds and raisins soaked in coffee. Since Chocolate and Cabernet Sauvignon have an affinity for each other, serve a slice of this torte with a glass of Cabernet Sauvignon.

Serves 8 to 10

¼ cup raisins	⅔ cup sugar
¼ cup hot coffee	⅔ cup ground almonds
10 ounces semi-sweet chocolate	4 tablespoons sifted cake flour
12 tablespoons (1 ½ sticks) butter, softened	1 teaspoon vanilla extract
4 large eggs, separated	½ teaspoon almond extract

Butter and flour a 9-inch torte or springform pan. Soak the raisins in the hot coffee. Melt the chocolate and beat it together with the butter. Beat the egg yolks and the sugar together. Add the raisins and coffee to the egg mixture. Stir in the ground almonds, cake flour, vanilla and almond extracts. Then blend in the chocolate mixture. Beat the egg whites until stiff and fold them into the batter.

Pour the batter into the prepared pan and bake in a preheated 375° F. oven for 30 to 35 minutes or until the top springs back when lightly touched. When cool, glaze the cake.

Glaze

6 tablespoons butter	3 tablespoons brandy
3 tablespoon light corn syrup	4 ounces semi-sweet chocolate

Melt the butter, corn syrup, brandy, and chocolate over medium heat, stirring well to combine. Gently pour the glaze over the cake. Some of the glaze will run down the sides.

Chambourcin

This French hybrid was developed by Joannes Seyve (1900-1966), younger brother of the more famous French hybridized, Bertille Seyve, and released for commercial cultivation in 1963. It became popular with vintners in the Loire Valley of France where half of the world's Chambourcin is planted. The vines grow aggressively and have good resistance to disease. The varietal grape has a nice crimson color and produces a simple wine with noticeable aroma and herbaceous flavor. Although some French vintners finish it as a rosé, most make Chambourcin into a red wine which they age in oak barrels.

There are five producers of Chambourcin varietal wine in Virginia: Burnley Vineyards near Charlottesville, Deer Meadow near Winchester, Stonewall Vineyard near Appomattox, Chateau Morrisette on the Blue Ridge Parkway, and North Mountain Vineyard & Winery in the Shenandoah Valley. Lee Reeder at Burnley calls his 100 percent Chambourcin wine Rivanna Sunset, while Dick McCormack at North Mountain calls his Virginia Claret. Stonewall, long a recognized producer of a Chambourcin wine, lightly presses the grapes and ferments the wine on the skins, following which the wine is aged in oak barrels for two years.

Savoy Pork Chops

In this recipe of French origin the mild flavor of pork chops is enhanced by savoy cabbage to which juniper berries have been added. Although this dish is prepared with white wine, it pairs well with a light red wine, such as Chambourcin.

Serves 4

1 small head savoy cabbage, cored and
    shredded
5 tablespoons butter
1 onion, finely chopped
1 clove garlic, finely chopped
Salt and pepper

4 juniper berries, crushed
4 medium-thick pork chops
1 ¼ cups dry white wine
2 tablespoon fine dry white bread crumbs
2 tablespoon grated Gruyere cheese

Blanch the cabbage in boiling water for 3 minutes and then drain it well. Melt 2 tablespoons of the butter in a large skillet over medium heat. Add the onion and garlic and sauté until softened. Then add the cabbage and season it lightly with salt and pepper. Stir in the juniper berries and remove the cabbage from the pan and set aside.

Season the chops with salt and pepper. Melt another 2 tablespoons of butter in the skillet and when the butter is hot add the pork chops and brown them on both sides.

Put half of the cabbage mixture in an ovenproof casserole, lay the pork chops on top, side by side, and cover with the remaining cabbage. Pour the wine into the skillet and bring quickly to a boil, stirring in any browned particles in the skillet. Boil for 1 minute to reduce the liquid slightly and then pour over the cabbage. Sprinkle with the bread crumbs mixed with the cheese, dot with the remaining butter. Bake in a preheated 375° F. oven for 40 to 50 minutes or until golden brown.

Sautéed Rabbit with Peppers

The use of red and chili peppers, in addition to the olives and capers, give this dish a piquant flavor. Serve this rabbit dish with a light red wine, such as Chambourcin.

Serves 6

2 medium-sized fryer rabbits, cut into
    serving pieces
Salt and pepper
Flour
3 tablespoons vegetable oil
1 large onion, sliced
3 cloves garlic, chopped
2 red bell peppers, peeled, seeded, and sliced

1 hot chili pepper, seeded and deveined,
    or ¼ teaspoon red pepper flakes
1 cup sherry
¾ cup chicken broth
½ teaspoon dried thyme
¼ cup sliced black olives
2 tablespoons capers

Season the rabbit with salt and pepper and dust lightly with flour, shaking off the excess.

Heat the oil in a Dutch oven or large heavy skillet with a lid. Add the rabbit pieces and the onion and sauté until they are browned. Stir in the garlic and peppers, combing them with the contents of the skillet. Add the sherry, broth, and thyme, bring to a boil and then lower heat to a simmer. Cook covered over low heat for 30 to 35 minutes or until the rabbit is tender. Sprinkle on the olives and capers and continue cooking for another 10 minutes. If the sauce has not thickened, cook over medium heat uncovered for the last ten minutes to reduce the juices.

de Chaunac

Another red French hybrid developed by the prolific hybridizer, Albert Seibel, around the turn of the century. De Chaunac is early ripening, highly productive and resistant to disease. The grape produces a full-bodied red wine with strong color. If kept on the skins for more than a short time, de Chaunac wine exhibits an unpleasant vegetal aroma and flavor.

Meredyth Vineyards in northern Virginia is the only Virginia winery offering a varietal de Chaunac wine.

Country Captain Chicken

The recipe for Country Captain Chicken was brought to Savannah, Georgia, in the 1700s by a sea captain who was involved in the spice trade. There have been many variations since then. The spiciness of the dish depends on the amount of curry powder used. Some cooks use a stewing hen and let it cook for several hours.

Serves 4

½ cup flour
¾ teaspoon salt
½ teaspoon black pepper
½ teaspoon paprika
1 (3 pound) chicken cut-up
2 tablespoons butter or margarine
2 tablespoons vegetable oil
1 large onion, chopped
1 green pepper, chopped

2 small cloves garlic, minced
3 tablespoons chopped parsley
1 tablespoon curry powder
¼ teaspoon dried thyme
1 (16 ounce) can tomatoes
1 teaspoon Tabasco sauce or 1 small jalapeno
    pepper, seeded and chopped
½ cup dried currants
¾ cup toasted slivered almonds.

Combine the flour, salt, pepper, and paprika and dredge the chicken pieces in the seasoned flour. Heat the butter and oil in a large heavy skillet over medium-high heat. Sauté the chicken pieces until golden brown and then remove them to a plate.

Discard all but 2 tablespoons of the drippings from the skillet. Add the onions, pepper, and garlic and sauté over medium-low heat until the vegetables start to soften, about 5 minutes. Add the parsley, curry powder, thyme, tomatoes, and Tabasco sauce. Return the chicken to the pan and spoon some sauce over the chicken. Cover and cook on low heat for 30 minutes. Add the currants, re-cover and cook for another 30 minutes of until the chicken is tender. Sprinkle the chicken with the toasted almonds and served with boiled rice.

Gnocchi with Herb Sauce

Gnocchi are small Italian dumplings. These differ from the traditional ones in that they are made with cheese instead of potatoes. The gnocchi may be made ahead and frozen.

Serves 6 as a first course

1 pound ricotta cheese	1 ¾ cups flour
1 egg, beaten	1 tablespoon vegetable oil
¼ teaspoon salt	Freshly grated Parmesan cheese

In a bowl mix together the ricotta cheese, egg, salt, flour, and oil to form a dough. Cut or tear off small pieces of the dough and roll them with your hands on a floured board until the pieces are the size of bread sticks. Then cut these sticks into 1-inch pieces and curl them slightly. Place the gnocchi on a floured sheet of wax paper and refrigerate until ready to use.

Herb Sauce

2 tablespoons olive oil	1 can (1 pound) tomatoes, diced with juice
¾ cup chopped onions	3 tablespoons each of chopped fresh sage,
1 clove garlic, minced	chopped fresh rosemary, and chopped
1 can (8 ounces) tomato sauce	fresh thyme

Heat the oil in a medium-size saucepan over medium heat. Add the onions and garlic and sauté until the onions are soft. Add the remaining sauce ingredients and simmer uncovered, stirring occasionally, for 30 minutes.

Heat lightly salted water in a large saucepan to the boiling point. Drop the gnocchi into the boiling water and cook until they float to the surface, 3 to 5 minutes. Remove with a slotted spoon and let them drain in a colander for a few minutes. Then serve the gnocchi with the Herb Sauce and grated Parmesan cheese.

Gamay

The Gamay grape is so closely associated with the Beaujolais region of France that many wine drinkers erroneously assume that the name of the grape is Gamay Beaujolais. The Beaujolais region is intensely committed to Gamay as it represents well over 95 percent of the vines in the region. It is one of France's everyday wines and is enjoyed young when vinified in the popular nouveau style, which ferments whole grapes in the macération carbonique technique that minimizes extraction of tannins. A number of vintners in the Beaujolais region also produce a more traditional style of Gamay which requires aging in oak barrels to be enjoyed. The wine is light purple in color, has high acid, and intense fruity aroma.

Loudoun Valley Vineyards is the only producer of Gamay grapes in Virginia. Hubert Tucker, owner of Loudoun Valley, produces his Gamey wine in the nouveau style traditional in the Beaujolais region.

Orange Chicken

Orange juice and chili sauce flavor this oven baked chicken which is reminiscent of a lightly-spiced barbecued chicken. Salt and pepper the chicken before flouring it, if desired.

Serves 4

1 frying chicken (3 ½ pounds), cut up
⅓ cup flour
¼ cup vegetable oil
1 cup fresh orange juice
½ cup chili sauce
1 tablespoon brown sugar

1 tablespoon maple flavored pancake syrup
¼ cup chopped green pepper
1 teaspoon prepared mustard
1 clove garlic, minced
2 tablespoons soy sauce
2 medium oranges, peeled and sliced

Wash and dry chicken pieces. (The chicken pieces may be skinned, if desired.) Roll them in the flour. Heat the oil in a skillet, add the chicken and brown lightly on all sides. Remove the chicken pieces to a flat open baker. Drain the fat from the skillet and add the remaining ingredients, except the orange slices. Simmer the mixture for 2 to 3 minutes to blend flavors. Pour the sauce over the chicken. Cover the dish with aluminum foil and bake in a preheated 350°F. oven for 50 to 60 minutes or until the chicken is done. Just before serving add the orange slices.

Shoulder Roast of Veal with Fennel and Mushrooms

This recipe utilizes the less expensive shoulder roast of veal. It is cooked with sautéed mushrooms and fennel in a tomato-wine sauce. Serve the roast with either small pasta or rice. This recipe makes an easy entree for a dinner party.

Serves 8

1 (4 pound) shoulder roast of veal	1 carrot, chopped
Salt, pepper, garlic powder, to taste	1 small onion, chopped
2 tablespoons olive oil	1 large fresh tomato, finely chopped
1 tablespoon butter or margarine	1 cup dry white wine
1 large fennel bulb, trimmed	½ cup chicken broth
½ cup sliced shiitake mushrooms	⅓ cup freshly chopped basil
¾ cup sliced white or crimni mushrooms	1 tablespoon of dry Italian seasonings
1 leek white, white part only, thinly sliced	¼ cup cream, optional

Sprinkle the roast on both sides with salt, pepper, and garlic powder, to taste. Heat the oil and butter in a large deep ovenproof skillet over medium heat until the butter starts to foam. Add the roast and brown it on both sides over medium heat.

Trim the tough end off the fennel, cut it in half and then slice it thinly. When the roast has browned remove it from the skillet and add the fennel, mushrooms, leek, carrot and onion. Sauté over medium heat until the vegetables start to become limp. Add the tomato and sauté for a few minutes longer. Then add the wine and chicken broth and mix well. Push some of the vegetables aside in the center of the pan to make room for the roast. Return the roast to the pan, baste with some of the juices, and sprinkle the basil and herbs on top. Bake, covered, in a preheated 325° F. oven for 1 ¾ to 2 hours or until the meat is tender.

Remove the meat to a warm platter, add the cream, if desired, and reduce the gravy slightly over medium-high heat. Cut the meat into slices and serve with pasta and spoon some gravy and vegetables over the meat and pasta.

Malbec

Also called Cot after a river in the Bordeaux region of France, Malbec is used primarily as a blending wine with Cabernet Sauvignon by Bordeaux vintners. It is low in acid and, therefore, early maturing. The wine from Malbec grapes is moderately bodied, and frequently has an undertone of strawberries or blackberries. One of its disadvantages, at least in the Bordeaux region, is that the vines have a tendency to coulure (fail to bloom).

Horton Vineyards in Orange county has recently introduced a varietal wine from the Malbec grape, the only Virginia vintner to make a Malbec wine. In fact, Horton is one of only three or four wineries in the United States to be producing this varietal wine. Tony Bieda, general manager of Horton Vineyards, says they leave the grapes on the skins for several weeks to give the wine deep color, and then rack it off into oak barrels where it is left for 12-14 months of aging.

Five Spice Beef

This oven-braised beef recipe includes Chinese five-spice powder, which consists of equal amounts of cloves, cinnamon, fennel seeds, star anise, and Szechuan peppercorns. Since this dish needs no last minute preparation, it is an ideal one to include in a Chinese meal.

Serves 4 or 6 to 8 with other Chinese dishes

2 tablespoons peanut oil
1 ½ pounds lean stewing beef, cut into cubes
1 ¾ cups beef broth
¼ cup low sodium soy sauce
3 tablespoons sherry
2 tablespoons sugar

4 slices fresh ginger, minced
2 cloves garlic, minced
2 teaspoons Chinese five-spice powder
2 cups thickly sliced fresh mushrooms
1 tablespoons cornstarch mixed with
    2 tablespoons cold water

Heat the oil in a Dutch oven medium-high heat. Add the meat and brown it on all sides. Stir in the beef broth, soy sauce, sherry, sugar, ginger, garlic, five-spice powder, and mushrooms. Bring the mixture to a boil, cover the pan, and cook in a preheated 325° F. oven for 1 ½ hours or until the meat is tender. Skim the fat from the sauce and thicken with the cornstarch mixture, adding it slowly until the desired thickness is achieved. Serve with steamed rice.

Chicken in Peanut-Tomato Sauce

This Chicken in Peanut-Tomato Sauce has an interesting sweet and sour flavor as well as the spiciness of chili powder. If desired, the chicken may be skinned before cooking. Serve this dish with rice and a green vegetable along with a glass of Malbec.

Serves 4

1 (3 to 3 ½ pound) frying chicken, cut-up	¼ cup peanut butter
½ teaspoon salt	1 can (8 ounces) tomato sauce
¼ teaspoon pepper	⅓ cup dry white wine
2 tablespoons vegetable or olive oil	⅓ chicken broth
1 medium onion, chopped	1 tablespoon sugar
1 clove garlic, chopped	1 tablespoon vinegar
½ cup chopped green pepper	1 teaspoon chili powder

Wash and dry the chicken and sprinkle it with salt and pepper. Heat the oil in an oven-proof skillet, add the chicken pieces and brown them on both sides. Remove the chicken and add the onion, garlic, and green pepper. Sauté until the onion is lightly browned. Blend in the remaining ingredients and add the chicken pieces. Cover and bake in a preheated 325° F. oven for 50 minutes. Serve chicken with the sauce.

Maréchal Foch

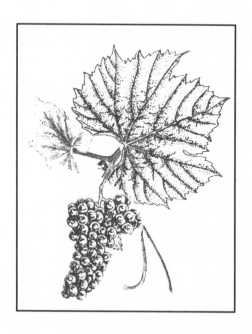

This red French hybrid was developed by a leading French hybridizer, Eugene Kuhlmann (1858-1932), who released it in France following World War I. Surprisingly, one of its parents is a white hybrid, Goldreisling, which has among its parents, Riesling and Muscat. Maréchal Foch ripens early and is fairly tolerant of cold winters. The wine produced by the Foch grape has strong color and flavor, reminiscent of a burgundy. The intense flavor is frequently attenuated by oak aging, or by fermenting the grape in the nouveau style (carbonic macération technique).

While several other wineries grow Maréchal Foch and use it in their blended wines, only three wineries produce a varietal Maréchal Foch wine. These are Deer Meadow in the northern Shenandoah Valley, Meredyth Vineyards near Middleburg, and Rose Bower Vineyard & Winery near Hampden-Sydney. Charles Sarle at Deer Meadow ages his Maréchal Foch and achieves what he believes is a balanced wine with cinnamon and berry undertones. Archie Smith III at Meredyth brings out the ruby-red color that is characteristic of the Maréchal Foch grape by extended skin contact. He calls his Maréchal Foch varietal wine Honeysuckle Rose. Tom O'Grady at Rose Bower makes his Maréchal Foch in the style of a nouveau Beaujolais, and calls it Maréchal Foch Autumn Wine.

Lentil Soup with Meatballs

Lentils were brought to America by Jesuit missionaries who first planted them along the St. Lawrence River. Today they are grown in a 50-mile-wide strip of land along the Idaho-Washington border. The arid climate of this region makes it possible to dry lentils in the field before harvesting. This Lentil Soup with Meatballs is a hearty main course and needs only a green salad as an accompaniment. Ground beef may be substituted for the lamb, if desired.

Serves 4

¾ pound lentils, picked over and rinsed
2 stalks celery, sliced
2 carrots, diced
¾ cup sliced mushrooms
1 medium onion, chopped
⅓ cup barley
2 tablespoons chopped fresh dill
¼ teaspoon pepper
1 (1 pound) can tomatoes
4 cups chicken broth
3 cups water

¾ pound lean ground lamb
½ teaspoon onion powder
½ teaspoon salt
¼ teaspoon pepper
¼ teaspoon dried thyme
1 egg
2 tablespoons bread crumbs
2 tablespoons olive oil
⅓ cup elbow macaroni or small pasta
1 ½ cups shredded kale

Combine the lentils, celery, carrots, mushrooms, onion, barley, dill, and pepper in a soup pot. Chop the tomatoes into small pieces and add them, their juice, the chicken broth, and water to the soup pot. Bring to a boil, reduce heat and cook, covered, over low heat for 1 ½ hours.

Combine the lamb, onion powder, salt, pepper, thyme, egg, and bread crumbs in a mixing bowl. Then shape the mixture into 12 meatballs. Heat the oil in a skillet, add the meatballs, and brown them on all sides. Remove the meatballs with a slotted spoon and add them, the pasta, and the kale to the soup. Cook on medium low for 20 minutes. Serve immediately.

Oriental Flank Steak with California Pasta Salad

This recipe utilizes a less expensive cut of beef and marinates it in a sauce, which gives the steak an oriental flavor. For a barbecue serve the steak and salad with Maréchal Foch wine.

Serves 4

1 large flank steak, about 2 pounds
2 tablespoons oil
¼ teaspoon sesame seeds
½ teaspoon garlic powder
½ teaspoon onion powder
⅛ teaspoon ground cloves

2 teaspoons fresh chopped ginger
5 tablespoons soy sauce
5 tablespoons orange juice concentrate
5 tablespoons brandy
Coarsely ground pepper, to taste

Score the flank steak on both sides and place in a shallow pan. In a small bowl combine the remaining ingredients and pour them over the steak. Marinate the steak in the refrigerator for 4 hours, turning the steak occasionally. Broil on the grill for 4 to 5 minutes per side for medium. Slice thinly across the grain at a 45° angle.

California Pasta Salad

8 ounces fusilli (corkscrew pasta)
1 tablespoon extra virgin olive oil
2 medium tomatoes, blanched, peeled,
    and seeded
¼ cup sliced black olives

½ cup sliced celery
⅓ cup chopped red pepper
¾ cup blanched broccoli florets
2 jalapeño peppers, seeded and finely chopped
2 teaspoons chopped fresh cilantro leaves

Cook the fusilli in boiling salted water until al dente, rinse in cold water and drain. Transfer the pasta to a serving dish and toss with the olive oil. Chop the tomatoes into bite-size pieces and add them with the olives, celery, red pepper, broccoli, chili peppers and chopped cilantro to the pasta. Toss well to combine. Pour the dressing over the salad and combine well. Refrigerate until serving time, at least one hour, to blend the flavors.

Dressing

1 tablespoon white wine vinegar
1 ½ tablespoon lime juice
½ teaspoon Dijon mustard

Dash of garlic powder
½ teaspoon cayenne pepper
5 tablespoons extra-virgin olive oil

In a small bowl, whisk together the vinegar, lime juice, mustard, garlic powder, and cayenne pepper. Gradually add the oil, while continuing to whisk.

Merlot

Merlot is a fine red wine grown extensively in the Bordeaux region of France. Its origin is uncertain as its first mention in history is in the Bordeaux region as recently as the eighteenth century. Traditionally, Merlot has been thought of as an important blending wine with Cabernet Sauvignon to soften the latter's aggressiveness. In recent years, however, it has also become an established varietal wine in its own rights. Merlot is now grown extensively in southern Europe, particularly Hungary, Romania, Slovania, and Bulgaria, as well as in California and Washington in the United States.

More than one wine writer has described Merlot as one of the world's most underrated wines. It has somewhat the same herbaceous aromas as Cabernet Sauvignon, but has a lusher fruitiness and contains much softer tannins. Merlot's fruitiness and soft tannins allow it to be approachable after a shorter period of aging than its elegant neighbor, Cabernet Sauvignon. In cooler climates, such as northern Italy and Switzerland, Merlot is considered a wine to be drunk young with almost no aging.

Merlot appears to be doing well in Virginia with twelve wineries currently offering it as a varietal wine. Virginia vintners are generally treating Merlot in the traditional Bordeaux style, both as a blending agent with Cabernet Sauvignon and as a varietal wine. While Montdomaine Cellars was the first winery to gain special recognition for its fine Merlot, other wineries are now offering medal-winning Merlot as well.

Taco Salad

Mexican seasonings and cool crunchy lettuce abound in this hearty salad, which is ideal fare for a warm summer evening. Serve with a glass of Merlot.

Serves 4 to 6

1 pound lean ground beef
1 medium onion, chopped
1 can (8 ounces) tomato sauce
½ cup water
1 teaspoons chili powder
1 ½ teaspoons Mexican seasonings
½ teaspoon cumin
1 can (16 ounces) kidney beans
⅛ teaspoon crumbled red pepper flakes
½ medium head lettuce, torn into
     bite-size pieces

2 medium tomatoes, cut into chunks
½ medium green pepper, chopped
¼ medium red pepper, chopped
1 can (2.2 ounces) sliced black olives
1 Haas avocado
¾ cup shredded sharp Cheddar cheese
¾ cup shredded Monterey Jack cheese
1 cup broken corn chips
Additional corn chips
Bottled taco sauce, optional

Cook the beef and onions in a large skillet over medium-high heat until the meat is no longer pink. Drain any accumulated fat. Add the tomato sauce, water, chili powder, Mexican seasonings, cumin, and kidney beans, which have been drained and rinsed. Stir well to combine and cook over low heat for 10 to 15 minutes until the sauce is smooth, stirring occasionally.

Gently combine the lettuce, green and red peppers, olives, and avocado in a large bowl. Spoon the sauce over the lettuce. Top with the cheeses and then corn chips. Serve immediately and pass additional corn chips and taco sauce, if desired.

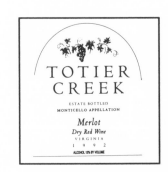

Hungarian Goulash with Spätzle

In many European homes this goulash is traditionally made with equal amounts of veal, pork, and beef. Serve over spätzle, which are small dumplings that originated in southern Germany, Austria and Hungary. Depending on where the recipe comes from, the spätzle dough may be made thick enough to roll out and cut into slivers, or thin enough to push through a colander.

Serves 6 to 8

2 tablespoons butter
3 pounds of veal stew, cut into
    1 to 2 inch pieces
4 slices bacon, cut into 1 inch pieces
1 large onion, cut in half and sliced
2 tablespoons flour

2 ½ tablespoons Hungarian paprika
½ teaspoon black pepper
1 teaspoon caraway seeds
1 ½ cups beef broth
1 cup sliced mushrooms, domestic white
    and shiitake

In a Dutch oven over medium high heat melt the butter and swirl it around so that it covers the bottom of the pan. Add the veal, bacon, and onions, and lower the heat to medium. Sauté, stirring occasionally, until the veal looses its color. Sprinkle the flour over the meat and mix well. Then add the paprika, pepper, and caraway seeds and combine them with the meat. Gradually add the beef broth, stirring to blend, so that there will be no lumps of flour. Add the mushrooms. Cover the Dutch oven and place in a preheated 325° F. oven for 1 ½ hours. Thicken the gravy with a little flour and water, if desired. Serve over spätzle.

Spätzle

3 eggs
1 ½ cups flour
½ cup milk

Dash each of salt, pepper, and nutmeg
3 tablespoon butter

In a bowl combine the eggs, flour and milk to form a medium-thick batter. Add the salt, pepper, and nutmeg. Bring lightly salted water to a boil in a large pot. When the water is boiling, place some of the batter on a small cutting board. Cut slivers of the dough and push them into the boiling water. Continue until all of the dough has been used. When the spätzle rise to the surface, cook for an additional minute or two. With a slotted spoon remove them from the water to a plate to dry slightly.

The spätzle may be kept warm in a low temperature oven. Place the spätzle into a shallow pan and drizzle a little melted butter over them to keep them from drying out.

Marinated Flank Steak with Potato Salad

The flank steak is marinated in a combination of onion, garlic, ginger, soy sauce, and honey. These oriental flavors pair well with the Russian-inspired potato salad. Enjoy with a glass of Merlot.

Serves 4

1 (1 ½ to 2 pounds) flank steak	¼ cup soy sauce
1 medium onion	3 tablespoons honey
2 cloves garlic	2 tablespoon peanut oil
1 (2-inch) piece fresh ginger	

Trim any existing fat from the flank steak and score it diagonally on one side, barely cutting through the meat into 2-inch diamonds. Cut the onion and ginger in large pieces and combine them with the garlic in the bowl of a food processor. Process until the mixture is the consistency of fine pieces. Combine the soy sauce, honey, and peanut oil and add the onion mixture. Place the flank steak in a zip-lock bag and add the marinade spreading it well on both sides of the meat. Close the bag and refrigerate for 24 hours.

Grill the meat over hot charcoals for about 3 minutes on each side for medium rare. Cut the meat on the diagonal and serve immediately with the potato salad.

Potato Salad

2 medium beets	6 tablespoons olive oil
1 ¼ pounds red potatoes	3 tablespoons chopped fresh dill
4 tablespoons white wine vinegar	½ teaspoon caraway seeds
½ English cucumber,	Lettuce leaves
2 ½ teaspoons Dijon mustard	
1 teaspoon sugar	

Place the beets in a medium saucepan, cover with water and cook over medium heat until tender, about 30 to 35 minutes. When beets are cool enough to handle, peel them and cut into ¾-inch cubes. Place beets in a small bowl.

At the same time cut the potatoes into ¾-inch cubes and boil them in water until tender, about 18 to 20 minutes. Drain the potatoes and transfer them to a large bowl. Add 2 tablespoons of the vinegar and gently stir the potatoes to mix in the vinegar. Cut the cucumber into ¾-inch cubes and add to the potatoes.

Mix the remaining 2 tablespoons of vinegar with the mustard and sugar in a small bowl. Whisk in the oil and then add the dill and caraway seeds. Add just enough dressing to the beets to coat them. Add the remaining dressing to the potatoes and stir gently to combine. Chill beets and potatoes separately until ready to serve.

Just before serving, gently mix the beets into the potato salad. Serve potato salad on lettuce leaves.

Meat Loaf with Orange and White Scalloped Potatoes

The combination of beef, veal, and pork gives this meat loaf a complex flavor. Both tomatoes and milk are included for a moist meat loaf. Leftovers may be served either hot or cold for sandwiches. Bake the potatoes along with the meat loaf for an old-fashioned meal.

Serves 6 to 8

1 ½ pounds ground meat, consisting of ½ pound beef, ½ pound veal, and ½ pound pork	1 cup crushed soda crackers
	1 (8 ounce) can stewed tomatoes
	1 (5 ounce) can condensed milk
1 cup coarsely chopped fresh mushrooms	1 large egg
½ cup chopped celery	2 tablespoons ketchup
⅓ cup chopped red pepper	½ teaspoon salt
½ cup chopped green pepper	¼ teaspoon pepper
1 large onion, chopped	

In a large bowl lightly combine the meats, mushrooms, peppers, onion and soda crackers. Then add the stewed tomatoes with their juice, the milk, egg, ketchup, and salt and pepper. Mix lightly, but thoroughly. Turn the mixture into a flat casserole, shaping the meat loaf into a long mound. Bake in a preheated 350° F. oven for 1 hour and 15 minutes. Occasionally remove any accumulated liquid fat.

Orange and White Scalloped Potatoes

¾ pound sweet potatoes, peeled	1 ½ cups shredded Monterey Jack cheese
¾ pound white potatoes, peeled	1 teaspoon nutmeg
½ teaspoon powdered mustard	1 large egg
Salt and pepper, to taste	1 ½ cups milk
1 ½ tablespoon flour	2 tablespoons butter

Thinly slice both the sweet and white potatoes. Combine the mustard salt, pepper and flour in a small bowl.

Butter a 2-quart gratin or shallow baking dish and place half of the white potatoes in the dish. Sprinkle them with ½ cup of the cheese and ⅓ teaspoon of the nutmeg. Cover this layer with half of the sweet potatoes and sprinkle with half of the flour mixture. Repeat with two more layers, one of white and one of sweet potatoes.

Whisk the egg in a medium bowl. Scald the milk and then whisk it into the beaten egg in a slow stream. Pour this mixture over the potatoes and sprinkle the remaining cheese and nutmeg over the top. Flake the butter on top. Bake in a preheated 350° F. oven for 1 to 1 ¼ hours or until the potatoes are tender and the top of the dish is bubbling and brown.

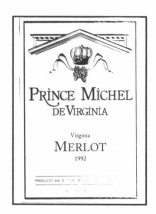

Mourvèdre

Mourvèdre is a red grape variety grown primarily in the south of France on the Côtes du Rhône and the Côtes du Provence. Mourvèdre is also grown in Australia, Spain, and California, where it is known as Matáro. The grape has a thick skin and is, therefore, somewhat resistant to mildew and other diseases common to hot, humid climes. The vines bud late so the variety is suitable to regions that experience late spring frosts. A full-bodied wine, Mourvèdre is traditionally used as a blending wine, although properly handled it can produce an intensely spicy wine with berry undertones.

Dennis Horton of Horton Vineyards is the only producer of Mourvèdre in Virginia, having planted seven acres in his vineyards near Orange in 1991. The wine was first released in 1994, based on the 1992 harvest. It contains approximately 10 percent of Syrah, which is traditionally done in France to provide additional tannins and an undertone of black pepper. In making the wine, Horton kept the grapes on the skins for one month to increase the varietal character and provide additional soft tannins. It was then pressed and place in oak barrels, where it was left to age for 18 months.

Chicken with Black Olive Stuffing

The stuffing of black olives, ham, bread, and green onions blends well with the lemon-rubbed chickens. Serve with a green vegetable for a company entree.

Serves 6

3 very small fryers (about 2 to 2 ½ pound)
1 lemon
4 slices dry bread, crumbled
3 tablespoon butter, melted, plus
    extra, softened, for cooking
4 green onions, chopped
½ cup ham, finely diced

⅓ cup black olives, coarsely chopped
2 tablespoon chopped parsley
1 tablespoon lemon juice
1 egg, slightly beaten
½ cup chicken broth
Salt and pepper, to taste

Cut each small fryer in half and rub inside and outside of the bird with a cut lemon.

In a bowl combine the bread, melted butter, green onions, ham, olives, parsley, lemon juice, egg, and chicken broth. Toss lightly to mix and season with salt and pepper, to taste.

Lightly rub a large flat ovenproof casserole or Pyrex pan with butter. Place six mounds of stuffing in the pan, spaced far enough apart to permit a half of the chicken to be placed on top. Place the cut half of the fryer on top of each mound of stuffing. Rub the top of each bird half with softened butter. Roast in a preheated 350°F. oven for 40 to 60 minutes, until done, depending on the size of the bird. With a spatula ease a bird half with its stuffing onto serving plates.

Fruit Stuffed Pork Chops with Country Potatoes

The fruity and spicy undertones of Mourvèdre complement the stuffing of these pork chops. Serve the chops with Country Potatoes for an old-fashioned meal.

Serves 4

4 very thick pork chops
1 Pippin or Granny Smith apple,
    peeled and grated
⅔ cup golden raisins
3 teaspoons grated orange peel
4 slices fresh ginger, each about ¼ inch thick,
    chopped

⅛ teaspoon ground cloves
Salt and pepper, to taste
3 tablespoons butter
½ cup dry white wine

Cut through the side of each chop to form a pocket for the stuffing.

In a bowl combine the apple, raisins, orange peel, ginger, cloves, and salt and pepper. Place equal amounts of this stuffing mixture into the pocket of each pork chop. Close the pocket with small skewers or toothpicks.

In a large skillet melt the butter and brown the pork chops on both sides. Add the wine. Cook the chops, covered, over low heat, turning the chops occasionally until done, about 35 to 40 minutes.

Country Potatoes

4 baking potatoes
⅔ cup chopped red pepper
1 medium onion, chopped

Butter
Pepper
Paprika

Peel the potatoes and slice them ¼-inch thick. Butter a 1 ½-quart casserole. Place a layer of potatoes in the casserole and sprinkle with some of the red pepper and onions. Dot with some butter flakes. Continue layering the potatoes, red pepper, and onions, and dotting them with butter until all of the ingredients are used. Sprinkle top with pepper and paprika. Cover casserole and bake in a preheated 400 F. oven for 1 hour. Uncover the casserole during the last 10 minutes of baking.

Nebbiolo

Nebbiolo is the varietal grape used in the finest red wines of the Piedmont region of northern Italy. Many wine experts consider Italian Nebbiolo wines as some of the finest red wines in the world. Its origin is traced back to the city of Alba in the thirteenth century. Nebbiolo grapes yield deep-colored wine with unusually high tannin and acid. The wine requires extensive aging to make it enjoyable. When mature the wine has a delightful scent and undertones suggesting violets or truffles.

Loudoun Valley Vineyards near Leesburg in northern Virginia is the only Virginia winery producing a Nebbiolo in the state.

Tomato-Cheese Pasta

One of the ingredients of this pasta sauce is a soft, mild, blue-veined cheese called Camenzola, also known as Cambuzola. If not available substitute the combination of Gorgonzola and Brie. The Brie will tone down the sharpness of the Gorgonzola. Serve this dish either as a main course, a first course, or as an accompaniment to grilled meats.

Serves 2

1 pound fresh tomatoes, cut in wedges
1 cup packed basil leaves
½ teaspoon garlic powder
6 ounces angel hair pasta

5 ounces Camenzola cheese or
   2 ounces Gorgonzola and 3 ounces
   ripe Brie, each cut into small cubes
Salt and pepper, to taste

Place the tomatoes, basil, garlic powder, and olive oil in the bowl of a food processor. Process until the ingredients are coarsely chopped, but not puréed.

Cook the pasta until it is al dente, about 4 to 5 minutes. Drain and place in a hot bowl. Add the cheese and stir well to melt the cheese and combine it with the pasta. Stir in the tomato mixture and serve at once.

Osso Buco à la Lombardy

Each region of Italy has its own version of Osso Buco (veal shanks) and this is an adaptation of the Lombardy style. Porcini mushrooms, tomatoes, and lemon zest flavor these veal shanks which pair well with a glass of Nebbiolo.

Serves 6

½ ounce dried porcini mushrooms
6 veal shanks, about 8 ounces each
3 tablespoons extra virgin olive oil
2 medium onions, chopped
1 stalk celery, finely chopped
1 small carrot, finely chopped

1 pound plum tomatoes, peeled and pureed
½ cup dry white wine
Zest of ½ lemon
Salt and pepper, to taste
2 tablespoons chopped Italian
     (flat-leaf) parsley

In a small bowl soak the mushrooms in hot water to cover for 30 minutes. Drain and squeeze out any excess water. Then chop the mushrooms and set them aside.

Heat the olive oil in a roasting pan over medium heat. Add the veal shanks and brown them on both sides. Then remove them from the pan and set them aside. Add the mushrooms, onions, celery, and carrot. Sauté just long enough to soften the vegetables. Then add the tomatoes, wine, and lemon zest and season with salt and pepper. Return the veal shanks to the pan, pushing them down into the vegetables and sauce. Bake, covered in a preheated 325° F. oven for 1 ½ hours, checking occasionally to see if more liquid is needed. If so add a little more wine.

Serve each veal shank covered with some of the vegetable mixture and pan juices and sprinkled with a little parsley.

Note: If dried porcini mushrooms are not available, sustitute shiitake and eliminate the soaking procedure.

Norton

The Norton grape variety is a natural cross between two native American species, Vitis Aestivalis *and* Vitis Labrusca. *It exhibits none of the foxiness of most* Labrusca-*based varieties. Norton is winter-hardy and disease-resistant. Its vines tend to grow extensively if not properly pruned and trained. The fruit achieves good sugar levels and is high in acid. The wine is darkly colored with a spicy flavor, some call it a coffee-like quality. The Norton grape is also called Cynthia, although some enologists consider them sisters rather than identical clones.*

The Norton grape was originally discovered by a Dr. Norton in Richmond around 1830. During the post-Civil War period and up to Prohibition, it was used to produce the famous Virginia Claret. This wine, produced principally by the Monticello Wine Company of Charlottesville, won awards at wine competitions both in the United States and Europe. By the end of Prohibition, all of the Norton vines in Virginia had been destroyed. However, vines had survived in neglected vineyards in Missouri and Arkansas. These vines were rehabilitated in the 1960s.

Horton Vineyards near Gordensville is the only grower and producer of Norton wine in Virginia. Cuttings for Dennis Horton's vineyard were obtained from the Norton vineyards in Missouri. Horton planted his Norton vineyard in 1990, and the Norton wine was first released in 1994, based on the 1993 harvest. This release was the first time since 1914, the year prohibition became law in Virginia, that wine from this native Virginia grape has been made commercially available in Virginia.

Mexican Chicken Casserole

This chicken casserole is a nice way to use leftover chicken. It is flavored with typical Mexican seasonings and pairs well with the full-bodied Norton wine.

Serves 4

1 can (14 ½ ounces) stewed tomatoes, Mexican style
½ teaspoon chili powder
1 teaspoon Mexican seasonings
¼ teaspoon oregano
2 cups cooked chicken, cut-up
½ cup chopped green pepper
½ cup chopped red pepper
1 jalapeño pepper, seeded and finely chopped

3 green onions, chopped
1 can (12 ounces) whole kernel corn
1 can (2.2 ounces) sliced black olives
1 ½ cups milk
2 tablespoons butter of margarine
½ cup cornmeal
1 cup grated Cheddar cheese
2 eggs, lightly beaten

Combine the tomatoes, chili powder, Mexican seasonings, and oregano in a saucepan. Bring to a slow boil and simmer for 10 minutes. Combine the chicken, peppers, onion, corn and olives in a bowl. Add the simmered tomato mixture and pour into a 3 quart casserole dish. (May be prepared ahead to this point and refrigerated. Bring to room temperature before proceeding.)

Heat the milk with the butter, then slowly add the cornmeal, stirring constantly to prevent lumps from forming. Cook over medium-low heat until thickened. Remove from heat; stir in the cheese and eggs. Pour over the chicken mixture, spreading it with a spatula to completely cover. Bake in a preheated 375° F. oven for 40 minutes or until the corn bread topping is done.

Barbecued Ribs

"A mess of barbecued ribs" was a meal always eagerly anticipated after hog butchering. Traditionally cooked over a hickory fire, the ribs were often basted with a tomato sauce to which bourbon had been added. This recipe uses a less alcoholic sauce.

Serves 4

1 side pork ribs (about 4 pounds)

Sauce

½ cup ketchup
⅓ cup light molasses
1 tablespoon light brown sugar
2 tablespoons orange juice
1 teaspoon grated orange zest
2 tablespoons vegetable oil

1 medium onion, finely chopped
1 clove garlic, minced
1 teaspoon prepared mustard
1 teaspoon Worcestershire sauce
⅛ teaspoon red pepper flakes
¼ cup bourbon

Place the side of ribs in a pan and bake in a preheated 350° F. oven for 45 minutes. Remove the ribs and discard the accumulated fat.

In the meantime combine all of the sauce ingredients in a saucepan. Bring the mixture to a slow boil and simmer for 15 minutes.

Place the ribs on the grill of a barbecue over slow coals, preferably hickory chips. Baste with the sauce and grill for about 45 minutes, or until done. Turn the ribs every 15 minutes and baste with the sauce. Cut the ribs into serving pieces and pass any leftover heated sauce.

Chili Verde with Corn Bread

Both green and jalapeño peppers are used in this Chili Verde. If a hotter chili is desired, add more jalapeno peppers and chili powder. Canned kidney beans may be added at the end of the cooking time. Finely-chopped red pepper and shredded Cheddar cheese add zest to the Skillet Corn Bread served with the Chili. The Norton wine complements the spices of the Chili.

Serves 6

Chili Verde

2 tablespoons vegetable oil
1 pound beef stew meat, cut into ¼-inch dices
1 pound lean pork, cut into ¼-inch dices
2 cloves garlic, minced
1 large onion, chopped
1 green pepper, chopped
2 jalapeño peppers, seeded and finely chopped
2 (1 pound) cans tomatoes, diced,
    juice reserved
1 (6 ounce) can tomato paste

¾ cup beef broth
¾ cup beer
⅓ cup chopped parsley
1 tablespoon chili powder
1 teaspoon ground cumin
¼ teaspoon ground cloves
Salt, to taste
1 or 2 (1 pound) cans kidney beans,
    drained, optional

Heat the oil in a Dutch oven, add the meats and brown them. Add the garlic, onion, and peppers and sauté until the peppers are soft. Add the tomatoes with their juice, tomato paste, beef broth, beer, parsley, chili powder, cumin, and cloves. Cook covered over low heat for at least two hours, stirring occasionally. Remove the cover, add beans, if desired, and simmer for another 45 minutes or until the mixture is thick. Season with salt, if necessary.

Skillet Cheddar Corn Bread

1 ½ cups yellow cornmeal
½ cup all-purpose flour
1 tablespoon sugar
1 tablespoon baking powder

½ teaspoon baking soda
1 cup milk
2 eggs, beaten
⅓ cup finely diced red pepper
1 ½ cups shredded Cheddar cheese

Preheat the oven to 425° F.. Thoroughly grease the bottom and sides of a 10-inch cast iron skillet and place it in the preheated oven while preparing the batter.

Combine the cornmeal, flour, sugar, baking powder, and baking soda in a mixing bowl. In another bowl combine the milk, eggs, diced red pepper, and cheese and add to the dry ingredients. Mix thoroughly and then pour the batter into the hot skillet. Bake in the preheated oven for 18 to 20 minutes until golden brown and a toothpick inserted in the center comes out clean. Cut into wedges and serve hot. Makes 8 to 10 wedges.

Veal Pot Roast

The use of veal instead of the traditional beef makes this a lighter-style pot roast. The slow cooking of both meat and vegetables produces a complex dish which is enhanced by the spices and complemented by the full-bodied Norton.

Serves 4

1 (3 to 3 ½ pound) bone-in veal shoulder roast
Salt and pepper
Garlic powder
Onion powder
Paprika
2 tablespoons olive oil
1 medium onion, chopped
1 cup white wine
1 cup chicken broth
1 cup sliced crimini mushrooms

¾ cup sliced shiitake mushrooms
3 carrots, cut in 2-inch chunks
1 medium tomato, cut into small chunks
6 to 8 small white potatoes
¾ teaspoon dried thyme
¾ teaspoon dried basil
½ teaspoon dried oregano
6 ounces green beans, trimmed and cut into 3-inch lengths
3 tablespoons flour combined with ½ cup water into a fluid paste

Sprinkle one side of the veal roast with salt, pepper, garlic powder, onion powder, and paprika. Heat the olive oil in a large, deep skillet (which has a lid) over medium heat. Add the veal, seasoned side down and brown it. Turn the meat to brown the other side and add the onions.

When the second side is brown add the wine and chicken broth. Then add the mushrooms, carrots, tomato, and potatoes, placing them around the roast, not on top of it. Sprinkle the meat and vegetables with the thyme, basil, and oregano. Cover and bake in a preheated 325° F. oven for 2 to 2 ¼ hours. Forty-five minutes before the end of the cooking time, add the green beans and continue cooking.

Remove the meat from the juice and thicken the gravy with some of the flour and water paste to the desired consistency. Serve meat with vegetables and gravy.

Pinot Noir

One of the oldest and outstanding wine grapes of the world, Pinot Noir is the source of the fine Burgundy wines of France. It is also an important ingredient in the champagne produced in the Champagne region. In the United States, Pinot Noir is produced mainly in California, Oregon, and Washington states. The Pinot Noir vines are very sensitive to soil and climatic conditions. The conditions in France that produce such complex and rich wines are proving hard to achieve in other parts of the world. In recent years, Oregon Pinot Noirs have become recognized as becoming the best that this country has to offer.

The wine from the Pinot Noir grape is difficult to characterize. There are at least 1,000 natural clones that have been identified from this ancient parent of Pinot Meunier, Pinot Grigio and Pinot Blanc (the latter frequently confused with Chardonnay). While the skin of the Pinot Noir grape is deep purple when ripe, the juice is white and historically was made into a white wine. Color is obtained by fermenting the juice on the skins.

The flavor of Pinot Noir wine can change with the locale, varying from pronounced berry tones to plum jam and even to earthy tones with almost no fruity character. Also, the character of the wine changes with aging, more so than perhaps any other wine. A mature Pinot Noir can take on a strong earthy aroma, even that of game or rotting vegetables.

Despite the difficulties in cultivating and vinifying Pinot Noir, there are seven intrepid vintners in Virginia engaged in doing just that. These are: Afton Mountain Vineyards, Barboursville Vineyards, Chateau Morrisette Winery, Jefferson (Simeon) Vineyards, Rockbridge Vineyards, Shenandoah Vineyards, and Tarara Winery. These vintners typically make their Pinot Noir in the traditional Burgundian manner, fermenting the juice on the skins and then aging the wine in oak barrels for approximately one year.

Pasta with Feta

Peperoncini are green chili peppers that are grown in the hotter climates of southern Italy. Traditionally used dried as a flavoring for stews and seafood, and in salami and sausages, the fresh pickled peperoncini are often a part of Italian anitpasto presentations and are also added to green salads. In this dish the peperoncini add a peppery accent to a tomato based pasta sauce. The pasta may also be served as a side dish to accompany grilled meats.

Serves 2 as an entree or 4 as a first course.

2 tablespoons olive oil
½ large red pepper, chopped
½ large green pepper, chopped
2 cloves garlic, diced
1 cup sliced crimini (brown) mushrooms
¼ cup thinly sliced and drained peperoncini

½ cup chopped fresh basil or
   2 tablespoons dried
1 (16 ounce) can tomatoes, diced, with juice
6 ounces fusilli (spiral-shaped pasta)
3 ounces crumbled feta cheese

Heat the oil in a skillet over medium heat. Add the peppers, garlic, and mushrooms and sauté until the vegetables begin to soften, about 4 minutes. Stir in the peperoncini, basil, and tomatoes with juice. Bring to a slow boil and then simmer until the sauce begins to thicken, about 5 minutes.

While preparing the sauce, cook the fusilli in boiling water until al dente. Drain the pasta well and add it to the sauce, stirring it gently to coat the pieces of pasta with the sauce. Add the feta cheese and stir to combine the mixture. Serve immediately.

Grilled Chicken with Mustard-Orange Glaze and Fluffy Spoon Bread

This grilled chicken is given a sweet and pungent flavor with orange juice, maple syrup, and two varieties of mustard. To give the entrée a Southern twist, serve it with Fluffy Spoon Bread.

Serves 4

1 (3 ½ to 4 pound) chicken, split for broiling
Salt, pepper, garlic powder, and onion powder, to taste
¼ cup fresh orange juice

2 tablespoons maple syrup or maple flavored pancake syrup
2 ½ teaspoons honey-orange mustard
2 ½ teaspoons coarse-grain mustard

Rinse the chicken and pat it dry. Sprinkle the outside with salt, pepper, garlic powder, and onion powder. Grill the two chicken halves over medium hot coals for 30 minutes.

In the meantime, combine the orange juice, maple syrup, and the two mustard in a small bowl. After 30 minutes of grilling time baste the chicken with the orange mixture and grill for another 10 minutes, then baste again and grill for another 10 minutes,. Repeat the basting process one more time for a total of 3 bastings and 30 more minutes of cooking time. Remove the chicken from the grill and cut it into serving pieces.

Fluffy Spoon Bread

1 ⅔ cups milk
¼ cup light cream
1 cup stone-ground white cornmeal
⅔ cup water
3 tablespoons soft butter

1 tablespoon sugar
Dash of salt
4 extra-large eggs, separated
2 teaspoons baking powder

In medium-size saucepan combine the milk, cream, cornmeal, water, butter, sugar, and salt . Bring to a slow boil over medium-low heat and then simmer for 2 minutes, stirring vigorously. Remove from heat and turn the mixture into a large bowl. Let it cool slightly.

Beat the egg whites until they hold stiff peaks. Beat the egg yolks with the baking powder until the yolks are light and lemon-colored. Stir the egg yolks into the cornmeal mixture quickly. Fold in a quarter of the egg whites and then fold in the remaining egg whites. Gently pour the batter into a greased 3-quart soufflé dish and bake in a preheated 375° F. oven for 35 minutes or until the top is lightly browned and a knife inserted in the center comes out clean. The center should still be soft and creamy. Spoon out individual servings at once and top with butter.

Moroccan-Style Cornish Game Hens with Bulgar

Orange, olives, and dates provide an enticing flavor for these Cornish game hens. This is an easy dish to prepare ahead-of-time as the hens should marinate at least overnight and then are just simply baked the next day.

Serves 4

1 large orange, thinly sliced
4 Cornish game hens, cut in half, lengthwise
6 tablespoons chopped fresh cilantro
½ teaspoon garlic powder
1 ½ teaspoons ground cumin
½ cup tawny port

¼ cup olive oil
2 tablespoons balsamic vinegar
2 tablespoons honey
12 whole pitted dates
10 large pitted green olives

Arrange orange slices in bottom of 9x13-inch glass baking dish. Top with the game hens. Mix the cilantro, garlic, cumin, port, and olive oil together in a bowl or measuring cup. Gently spoon the mixture over the hens. Tuck dates and olives between the hens. Cover and refrigerate overnight or 24 hours.

Then bake in a preheated 375° F. oven, basting occasionally for 50 minutes. Transfer hens, dates and olives to a platter. Pour pan juices into a small saucepan, remove fat and reduce slightly over medium heat. Spoon some sauce over the hens and serve with Bulgar.

Bulgar

1 ½ tablespoons olive oil
4 mushrooms, coarsely chopped
3 green onions, finely sliced
1 ¼ cup bulgar

2 tablespoons dried currants
1 ¼ teaspoon curry powder
2 ½ cups chicken broth

Heat the olive oil in a skillet over medium heat. Add the mushrooms and onions and sauté for 2 minutes. Stir in the bulgar, currants, curry powder, and chicken broth. Mix well. Bring the bulgar to a boil, cover and simmer for 20 minutes. Fluff with a fork before serving.

Duckling with Wild Rice Stuffing

This method of roasting a duck eliminates most of the fat from the bird during cooking. The crisp skin is basted with an orange-maple glaze and pineapple flavors the wild rice stuffing.

Serves 2

1 duckling (about 5 pounds)
Wild rice stuffing (recipe follows)
½ teaspoon salt
¼ teaspoon pepper
¼ teaspoon garlic powder

½ teaspoon onion powder
¼ teaspoon ground marjoram
½ teaspoon dry rosemary leaves
⅓ cup orange juice
⅓ cup maple syrup

Cut the wing tips off the duckling. Rinse the bird and pat it dry. Fill the cavity with the stuffing, packing it in rather tightly. Fold the rear skin flaps over each other and secure with metal skewers.

Place the duckling in a 13 x 9-inch glass baking dish. Sprinkle with the salt, pepper, garlic powder, onion powder, and marjoram. Crush the rosemary leaves as they are being sprinkled on top of the duckling. Bake in a 325° F. oven for 2 ¾ hours. About every 45 minutes, remove the accumulated fat with a bulb baster and loosen the back of the duckling if it has gotten stuck to the pan.

Combine the orange juice and maple syrup and generously baste the duckling. Increase oven heat to 350° F. and continue baking the bird for another 30 minutes, basting every 10 minutes (2 more bastings). Remove the duckling to a warm platter and cut into serving pieces. Serve with the wild rice stuffing.

Stuffing

¾ cup wild rice
¾ cup coarsely chopped mushrooms
1 small onion, chopped
1 stalk celery, chopped

⅓ cup chopped parsley
½ cup small fresh pineapple chunks
¼ teaspoon pepper
1 egg, lightly beaten

Place the rice in a small-holed colander and then put the colander in a bowl. Pour hot water over the rice, submerging it completely. Let the rice stand for 30 minutes, then drain. Repeat this process two more times. The rice kernels should begin to open.

Combine the rice with the rest of the stuffing ingredients.

Sangiovese

Sangiovese is the basis for the famous Italian Chiantis of Tuscany, where this varietal grape originated in ancient times. Tucsan Chiantis typically include a small amount of other red (and even white) wines. In recent years Cabernet Sauvignon has become a popular blending wine as it apparently fills in the weak spots in the Sangiovese taste spectrum.

The two producers of Sangiovese in Virginia are Hubert Tucker, owner of Loudoun Valley Vineyards near Leesburg in northern Virginia, and Gabriele Rausse at Jefferson (Simeon) Vineyards. Loudoun's first bottling of a varietal Sangiovese was from the 1992 harvest, which was released

in 1994, after two years of aging. Rausse released his 1993 harvest of Sangiovese in 1994.

Lentil and Lamb Soup

The combination of lamb and lentils in this hearty soup recipe is one of Basque origin. Serve the soup with a tossed salad and French bread.

Serves 6

1 pound lentils
8 cups water
1 teaspoon salt
½ teaspoon pepper
2 tablespoons butter or margarine
2 ½ cups canned, diced tomatoes, with juice
1 large onion, chopped
¼ cup chopped fresh dill

1 clove garlic, minced
½ bay leaf, crumbled
1 pound lean ground lamb
1 egg, slightly beaten
Flour
1 ½ tablespoon olive oil
¼ cup elbow macaroni

Wash the lentils and place them in a stock pot. Add the water, ½ teaspoon of the salt, ¼ teaspoon of the pepper, butter, tomatoes, onion, dill, garlic, and bay leaf. Bring to a slow boil and cook over low heat, covered for 1 to 1 ¼ hours or until the lentils are barely tender.

In the meantime combine the lamb with the remaining ½ teaspoon of salt, the remaining ¼ teaspoon of pepper, and the egg. Form into small meatballs and roll each in flour. Heat the olive oil in a large skillet and brown the meatballs. Then add them with the macaroni to the soup and continue cooking on low heat for 20 minutes.

Italian Beef Stew with Polenta

Both white and red wines are added to this Italian stew to give complexity to the gravy. A little pork also enhances the flavors of the stew. Serve the stew over polenta and accompany with steamed broccoli. Rice or pasta may be substituted for the polenta, if desired. A glass of Sangiovese pairs well with the stew.

Serves 6

2 ounces pancetta or lean bacon
1 carrot
1 stalk celery,
5 fresh sage leaves or 4 dried ones
2-inch sprig of rosemary or ½ teaspoon
    dried rosemary
4 to 5 tablespoons olive oil
1 ½ pound beef stew meat, cut into
    1 ½-inch cubes

½ pound lean pork, cut into 1 ½-inch cubes
½ cup dry white wine
3 onions, thickly slices
½ tablespoon sugar
Salt and pepper, to taste
1 ¼ cups red wine
Flour and water, to thicken gravy, optional

Chop together the pancetta, carrot, celery, sage leaves and rosemary needles until rather fine. Heat 2 tablespoons of the olive oil in a Dutch oven, add the vegetables and sauté until soft.

Heat another 2 tablespoons olive oil in a large skillet and brown the meat well on all sides. This may have to be done in several batches. Remove the meat from the skillet and place on top of the vegetables. Pour the white wine into the pan to deglaze it, scraping up any brown particles. Pour over the meat. Place the sliced onions on top of the meat and sprinkle with sugar, salt, and pepper.

Cover the Dutch oven and cook over low heat until the onion is wilted, about 10 minutes. Add the red wine. Place the covered Dutch oven in a preheated 325° F. oven for 2 hours or until the meat is fork tender. If desired thicken the gravy with a little flour and water mixed together. (1 part flour to 2 parts water)

Polenta

6 cups water
1 ¼ teaspoons salt

1 ½ cups coarse-grained yellow cornmeal
6 tablespoons butter, cut in 6 pieces

Bring the water and salt to a boil in a saucepan. Gradually whisk in the cornmeal. Stir briskly with a wooden spoon until the mixture boils and thickens, about 2 minutes. Reduce the heat to low, add the butter, a piece at a times, and continue stirring until it is melted and mixed with the polenta. Cook over low heat, stirring occasionally, for about 30 minutes. The polenta is cooked when it comes away cleanly from the sides of the pan. Pour the polenta on a large platter and spoon the Italian Beef Stew over it.

Stuffed Breast of Veal

In this recipe a breast of veal is baked with a light stuffing flavored with spinach, cheese, and herbs. Serve with a light red wine such as Sangiovese.

Serves 6

2 slices white bread, cubed
¾ cups milk
4 tablespoons butter or margarine
1 small onion, finely chopped
1 cup chopped spinach
⅔ cup grated Swiss cheese
1 cup mushrooms, coarsely chopped
¼ teaspoon nutmeg
½ teaspoon salt
¼ teaspoon pepper

2 tablespoons chopped parsley
3 tablespoons chopped fresh basil
1 boned breast of veal (about 4 pounds)
    with a pocket cut for stuffing
Salt and pepper, to taste
Paprika
1 cup chicken broth
½ cup white wine
⅓ cup whipping cream
2 tablespoons sour cream

Soak the bread in the milk in a bowl for 10 minutes and then squeeze dry. While the bread is soaking, heat 1 tablespoon of the butter in a small frying pan and sauté the onion until limp. Add the onion, spinach, cheese, mushrooms, nutmeg, salt, pepper, parsley, and basil to the soaked bread and mix gently. Lightly stuff the breast of veal and either sew the opening closed or secure it with metal skewers. Season the veal with salt and pepper and dust with paprika.

Heat the remaining 3 tablespoons of butter in a roasting pan over medium heat and brown the veal on the top side. Add the chicken broth and wine, cover the pan, and bake in a 325° F. oven for 1 ½ hours. Uncover the pan and bake for another 20 minutes.

Remove the veal to a platter and keep it warm. Skim any fat off the pan juices. Add the whipping cream and reduce to sauce consistency over medium heat or thicken with a combination of 2 tablespoons of flour dissolved in ¼ cup water. Blend in the sour cream. Slice the meat and serve with the sauce.

Syrah

Wine historians have placed the origin of the Syrah grape in the proximity of the Persian town of Shiraz, which is in the southeastern portion of what is now Iran. Historians are uncertain, however, as to how Syrah found its way to the Rhône Valley of France by Roman times. Its journey from France to Australia, where Syrah now comprises 40 percent of total plantings, has been pinpointed to a specific agriculturist who brought the plants to Sydney's Botanical Gardens in 1832.

Syrah vines are good grape producers where the climate is sufficiently warm, and are resistant to many wine grape diseases. The grapes produce a wine that has concentrated flavor, with undertones of pepper and spice, and high tannin. The latter requires extensive aging in oak to make the wine fully enjoyable. When suitably located, cultivated, and vinified, Syrah is considered one of the premium wines in the world.

Syrah has been introduced into Virginia only recently. Dennis Horton of Horton Vineyards first planted it in 1990 and released the 1992 vintage in late 1994. This first production was very small, although very rich in character, and is being sold only at the winery.

Grilled Short Ribs

The combination of stout and sugar helps tenderize beef short ribs. Although not usually considered to be a cut for barbecueing, these beef ribs are very tasty.

Serves 4

2 cups Guinness stout
1 large onion, sliced
⅓ cup soy sauce
⅓ cup brown sugar

¼ cup sesame oil
3 tablespoons minced garlic
3 to 3 ½ pounds beef short ribs,
    well trimmed

Whisk the first six ingredients together in a bowl. Place the ribs in a glass baking dish and pour the marinade over them. Cover and refrigerate overnight, turning the ribs once.

Glaze

½ cup marinade

3 tablespoon honey

Combine the glaze ingredients in a small bowl. Heat the grill to medium. Remove ribs from the marinade and place them on the grill. Grill until cooked through (about 30 minutes), brushing them with glaze as the ribs are turned.

Spaghetti with Cannellini

Cannellini are large, white Italian kidney beans. In this dish they and black olives are added to a light tomato sauce which is served over spaghetti. Accompany with a glass of Syrah.

Serves 4

1 tablespoon olive oil
8 ounces very lean ground beef
2 medium onions, chopped
1 small red pepper, chopped
1 small green pepper, chopped
1 small yellow pepper, chopped
Salt and pepper, to taste
1 tablespoon dried Italian herbs

1 can (28 ounces) tomatoes, chopped
    with juice
⅓ cup chicken broth
14 ounces thin spaghetti
½ cup chopped fresh basil
1 can (19 ounces) cannellini beans
1 can (2.2 ounces) sliced black olives, drained
1 tablespoon paprika

Heat the olive oil in a saucepan over medium heat. Add the ground beef, breaking it into small pieces as it cooks. Continue cooking until the meat is no longer pink. Then add the onions and peppers and sauté for 3 to 4 minutes. Season with salt, pepper, and the Italian seasonings. Add the tomatoes with their juice and the chicken broth and cook over medium-low heat for 10 to 15 minutes.

In the meantime, cook the spaghetti in boiling salted water until al dente. Drain and place in a bowl with 1 tablespoon olive oil and keep warm until the sauce is finished.

Rinse the beans and drain them. Add the basil, beans, olives, and paprika to the sauce and heat through. Pour the sauce over the spaghetti and serve.

Spicy Lamb Stew

Cinnamon, cloves, and coriander enhance this lamb stew, which also has a hint of citrus flavorings. Serve with a full-bodied red wine such as Syrah.

Serves 4

2 tablespoons olive oil	1 large strip lemon peel, cut in 4 pieces
2 pounds lamb stew, carefully trimmed and cut into 1 ½-inch cubes	1 cup red wine
	1 cup tomato juice
1 medium onion, chopped	½ teaspoon ground cloves
1 clove garlic, minced	½ teaspoon ground cinnamon
½ cup diced carrots	1 teaspoon powdered coriander
1 cup thickly sliced mushrooms	Flour and water, for thickening, optional
½ small orange, seeded and cut into 8 pieces	

Heat the olive oil over in a medium-size Dutch oven medium-high heat. Add the lamb and brown it. Add the onions, garlic, and carrots and sauté briefly. Then add the remaining ingredients. Cover and bake in a preheated 325° F. oven for 1 ½ to 2 hours or until the meat is tender. Check occasionally to see if more liquid is needed; if so add equal parts of wine and tomato juice. Remove any fat that may have accumulated on top of the stew and thicken with flour and water, if desired.

Villard Noir

This French hybrid, created in 1930, was developed from the Chancellor hybrid and another hybrid by the famous French hybridizer, Albert Seibel. Like its white sister, Villard Blanc, Villard Noir does well in warm climates where it yields a light-bodied, fruity everyday wine low in tannin.

In Virginia, Villard is generally used as a blending wine. Meredyth Vineyards is the only Virginia winery offering a varietal wine from the Villard Noir grape. Archie Smith at Meredyth calls the wine Honeysuckle Rose and adds a small amount of Riesling to give this blush wine some fruitiness.

Brunswick Stew

Although Brunswick County, Virginia, is supposed to be the birthplace of Brunswick Stew, almost every place named Brunswick from Georgia northward has claimed the origin of this dish. It was originally cooked all day in a big iron pot over the hearth. Brunswick Stew became a tavern favorite and is still frequently served at political functions. During colonial times squirrel was used to make the stew, but chicken has been substituted in modern times. Some Brunswick stews include beef and pork along with the chicken.

Serves 4

1 chicken (3 to 3 ½ pounds), cut-up
1 can (1 pound) tomatoes, chopped
1 large onion, sliced
1 cup cup okra pieces
1 cup lima beans
2 medium potatoes, peeled and diced

2 cups fresh or canned corn kernels
1 stalk celery, diced
¾ teaspoon salt
½ teaspoon pepper
⅛ teaspoon oregano
⅛ teaspoon thyme

Simmer the chicken in 4 cups of water, which has been lightly salted, for 1 hour or until the meat can easily be removed from the bones. Add the tomatoes and their juice, the vegetables and seasonings to the broth and simmer until the beans and potatoes are tender, about 25 to 30 minutes. Stir occasionally to prevent the vegetables from sticking.

In the meantime, remove the skin and chicken meat from the bones and cut the meat into bite-size pieces. When the vegetables are tender, add the chicken pieces, heat through, and serve.

Since long cooking improves the flavor of Brunswick stew, many cooks prefer to cook the stew one day and then slowly reheat and serve it the next day.

Cranberry and Turkey Pie

Turkey and cranberries are usually served together at Thanksgiving. This recipe combines leftover turkey with fresh cranberries in a deep dish pie, topped with puff pastry. Accompany with a glass of blush Villard Noir.

Serves 4 to 6

2 tablespoons butter or margarine
2 tablespoons flour
¾ cup chicken broth
¾ cup milk
1 ½ cups cooked turkey, cut into small pieces
8 ounces mushrooms sliced
2 stalks celery, chopped

8 ounces fresh cranberries
3 tablespoon medium sherry
½ cup light cream (half-and-half)
1 tablespoon lemon juice
1 package (17 ¼ ounces) frozen puff pastry sheets, thawed
1 egg, lightly beaten

Melt the butter in a large saucepan and stir in the flour to form a smooth paste. Gradually add the chicken broth and milk, stirring constantly to form a smooth sauce. Cook over low heat until the sauce begins to thicken. Remove from heat and add the turkey, mushrooms, celery, and cranberries. Then add the sherry, cream, and lemon juice. Stir the mixture and heat it gently just to warm through, without boiling.

Grease a deep 6-cup casserole or soufflé dish. Roll out the pastry to fit the top of the dish with a 1-inch overhang all around. Depending on the shape of the dish, the 2 pieces of puff pastry may have to be put together with gently strokes of a rolling pin. Gently pour the turkey mixture into the casserole and cover with the pastry. Crimp the edges of the pastry onto the edge of the dish to seal. Cut a small hole in the center of the pastry to allow steam to escape. Brush the pastry with the beaten egg and bake in a 375° F. oven for 30 to 35 minutes or until the pastry is brown. Serve immediately.

Zinfandel

Zinfandel is the mystery grape of the vinifera world, as its old-world source is unknown. Zinfandel is grown almost exclusively in California, where it is one of the most widely-planted grapes in the state. It produces the finest wine when grown in moderate climes, particularly in higher elevations which provide cool summer evenings.

Zinfandel is an ideal work-mate for California vintners as it can be used for a wide variety of wine products. As a white wine, for example it has been phenomenally successful. It has also been successfully produced as dry, sweet, fortified, or nouveau wines. Zinfandel has even been used as the basis of sparkling wines.

Because of its use in a variety of wine styles, it is not practical to describe Zinfandel's characteristic wine traits. As a dry wine, it does exhibit aromas of berries which become increasingly complex as the wine ages. Fermenting and aging Zinfandel in oak barrels also adds to the complexity of the wine.

As produced in Virginia, Zinfandel wine tends to be lighter-bodied then the full-bodied characteristics of California Zinfandels. Maturing of the vines and additional experience in vinification practices may strengthen the character of Virginia Zinfandel. There are currently two producers of Zinfandel in Virginia, Afton Mount Vineyards near Charlottesville, and Loudoun Valley Vineyards west of Leesburg. Hubert Tucker at Loudoun makes a red Zinfandel while Shinko Corpora at Afton immediately takes the juice off the skins and produces a semi-sweet white Zinfandel.

Fancy Mixed Grill

Three different meats, fruit, and vegetables are combined to make an unusual and flavorful dish. Serve with crusty French bread and a glass of Zinfandel.

Serves 8

Marinade

¾ cup vegetable oil
¾ cup red wine
⅓ cup low-salt soy sauce
2 tablespoons ketchup
3 teaspoons chopped fresh ginger

2 cloves garlic, minced
2 teaspoons curry powder
½ teaspoon pepper
¼ teaspoon Tabasco sauce

Blend all of the marinade ingredients in a food processor until smooth.

Kebobs

1 pound sirloin steak, cut into 2-inch pieces
1 pound boneless lamb, cut into 2-inch pieces
1 pound pork tenderloin, cut into
    2-inch pieces

12 large mushrooms
1 eggplant
4 firm Granny Smith apples
2 large green peppers

Place the meat in a bowl and pour the marinade over it. Cover and refrigerate for at least 24 hours.

One and a half hours before serving, prepare the vegetables. Wash and dry the mushrooms. Peel and slice the eggplant into 2-inch thick slices. Sprinkle them with salt and let them sit for 30 minutes. Then rinse the eggplant and pat dry with paper towels. Cut the eggplant slices into 2-inch cubes. Peel and core the apples and cut them into large wedges. Seed the peppers and cut them into 2-inch cubes. Place all of the vegetables in a bowl. Remove some of the marinade from the meat and add it to the vegetables, coating them well.

On large skewers, alternate the meats and vegetables, placing the apples in the middle. Barbecue on the grill or broil in the oven 5 to 7 minutes on each side.

Puffed Cinnamon-Apple Pancake

Cinnamon and tart apples make this brunch entrée extra delicious. Serve with white Zinfandel.

Serves 6

8 tablespoons butter	4 large eggs
¼ cup sugar	1 cup flour
2 teaspoons ground cinnamon	1 cup plus 2 tablespoons milk
2 large Granny Smith or Pippin apples, peeled, cored, and thinly sliced	1 teaspoon vanilla extract
	Powdered sugar

Melt the butter in a 10-inch skillet over medium-high heat. Stir in the sugar and cinnamon and mix well. Then add the apples and cook, stirring gently, until the apples are translucent, about 5 minutes. Place the skillet in a preheated 425° F. oven while quickly preparing the batter.

Beat the eggs in a bowl. Add the flour, milk, and vanilla, and beat until smooth. Pour the batter evenly over the apples in the pan. Bake until the pancake is puffy and golden, about 15 minutes. Sift powdered sugar over the pancake. Cut in wedges and serve immediately.

LOUDOUN
VALLEY

VIRGINIA
ZINFANDEL
(UNFILTERED)

PRODUCED & BOTTLED BY LOUDOUN VALLEY VINEYARDS
WATERFORD, VA. TABLE WINE

WINERY ADDRESSES

Afton Mountain Vineyards
Route 3, Box 574
Afton, VA 22920
(703) 456 8667

Autumn Hill Vineyards /
  Blue Ridge Winery
Route 1, P.O. Box 199 C
Stanardsville VA 22973
(804) 985 6100

Barboursville Vineyards
P.O. Box 136
Barboursville, VA 22923
(703) 832 3824

Burnley Vineyards
Route 1, Box 122
Barboursville, VA 22923
(703) 832 2828

Chateau Morrisette Winery
P.O. Box 766
Meadows of Dan, VA
24120
(703) 593 2865

Deer Mountain Vineyard
199 Vintage Lane
Winchester, VA 22602
(703) 877 1919

Dominion Wine Cellars
1 Winery Avenue
P.O. Box 1057
Culpeper, VA 22701
(703) 825 8772

Farfelu Vineyard
Route 1, Box 23
Flint Hill, VA 22627
(703) 364 2930

Gray Ghost Vineyards
Route 1, Box C 12-E
Amissville, VA 22002
(703) 937 4869

Guilford Ridge Vineyards
Route 5, Box 148
Luray, VA 22835
(703) 778 3853

Hartwood Winery
345 Hartwood Road
Fredericksburg, VA 22406
(703) 752 4893

Hollerith
(Not open to public)

Horton Vineyards &
  Winery
6399 Spottswood Trail
Gordonsville, VA 22942
(703) 832 7440

Ingleside Plantation
  Vineyards
Route 638, P.O. Box 1038
Oak Grove, VA 22443
(804) 224 8687

Jefferson Vineyards
Route 9, Box 293
Charlottesville, VA   22902
(804) 977 3042

Lake Anna Winery
5621 Courthouse Road
Spotsylvania, VA 22553
(703) 895 5085

Linden Vineyards
Route 1, Box 96
Linden, VA 22642
(703) 364 1997

Loudoun Valley Vineyards
Route 1, Box 340
Waterford, VA 22190
(703) 882 3375

Meredyth Vineyards
P.O. Box 347
Middleburg, VA 22117
(703) 687 6277

Misty Mountain Vineyards
SR 2, Box 458
Madison, VA 22727
(703) 923 4738

Montdomaine Cellars
Route 6, Box 188A
Charlottesville, VA 22902

Mountain Cove Vineyards
Route 1, Box 139
Lovingston, VA 22949
(804) 263 5392

Naked Mountain Vineyards
P.O. Box 131
Markham, VA 22643
(703) 364 1609

North Mountain Vineyard
& Winery
4613 Mount Vernon Mem.
Hwy
Alexandria, VA 22309
(703) 436 9463

Oakencroft Vineyard &
Winery
Route 5
Charlottesville, VA 22901
(804) 296 4188

Oasis Vineyard
Highway 635, Box 116
Hume, VA 22639
(703) 635 7627

Piedmont Vineyards and
Winery
P.O. Box 286
Middleburg, VA 22117
(703) 687 5528

Prince Michel Vineyards
HCR 4, Box 77
Leon, VA 22725
(703) 547 3707

Rebec Vineyards
Route 3, Box 185
Amherst, VA 24521
(804) 946 5168

Rockbridge Vineyards
P.O. Box 14
Raphine, VA 24472
(703) 377 6204

Rose Bower Vineyard and
Winery
P.O. Box 126
Hampden-Sydney, VA
23943
(804) 223 8209

Rose River Vineyards
Route 648, Box 186
Syria, VA 22743
(703) 923 4050

Shenandoah Vineyards
Route 2, Box 323
Edinburg, VA 22824
(703) 984 8699

Stonewall Vineyard
Route 2, Box 107A
Concord, VA 24538
(804) 993 2185

Swedenburg Estate Winery
US Route 50
Middleburg, VA 22117
(703) 687 5219

Tarara Vineyard and
Winery
13648 Tarara Lane
Leesburg. VA 22075
(703) 771 7100

Tomahawk Mill Winery
Route 3, Box 204
Chatham, VA 24531
(804) 432 1063

Totier Creek Vineyard
Route 6, Box 188-B
Charlottesville, VA 22902
(804) 979 7105

Villa Appalaccia
P.O. Box 734
Meadows of Dan, VA 24120

The Williamsburg Winery
2638 Lake Powell Road
Williamsburg, Virginia
23187
(804) 229 0911

Willowcroft Farm Vineyards
Route 2, Box 174-A
Leesburg, VA 22075
(703) 777 8161

Wintergreen Vineyards &
Winery
Route 664, Box 702
Nellysford, VA 22958
(804) 361 2519

Recipe Index